General Convention of the Christian Church

Christian Sunday School Hymnal

A Compilation of Choice Hymns and Tunes for Sunday Schools

General Convention of the Christian Church

Christian Sunday School Hymnal
A Compilation of Choice Hymns and Tunes for Sunday Schools

ISBN/EAN: 9783337428181

Printed in Europe, USA, Canada, Australia, Japan

Cover: Foto ©Thomas Meinert / pixelio.de

More available books at **www.hansebooks.com**

THE

CHRISTIAN

Sunday School Hymnal;

A COMPILATION

OF

CHOICE HYMNS AND TUNES

FOR

SUNDAY SCHOOLS.

CHRISTIAN PUBLISHING COMPANY,
913 PINE STREET.
ST. LOUIS. MO.

ELECTROTYPED BY
CAMPBELL & Co., 61 Longworth St.,
CINCINNATI, OHIO.

TRUSTEES' PREFACE.

————◦}◦○◑◦○◦{◦————

THE marked increase of interest in the Sunday School work within the past few years, has produced an unprecedented activity in the publication of Sunday School music books. Many of these, by reason of the transient character of the music and words employed, have proved short-lived. The schools soon tired of them, and demanded new books, which, in turn, ran their brief course to give place to others. Besides the expense involved in these frequent changes of music books, a worse evil, perhaps, was the inculcation of unscriptural sentiments which many of the popular songs contained, and the formation of wrong musical tastes. It was this state of things that led the General Convention, assembled at Louisville, in October, 1880, to adopt the following recommendation of a committee appointed to consider, and report on, the revision of the Hymnal:

"It is, furthermore, the judgment of your Committee that the preparation and publication, under the supervision of the Hymn Book Committee, of a Sunday School Hymnal, with a view of adjusting the singing in our Sunday Schools, as far as possible, to that in the church, and to prevent the frequent changes in music books, which is a source of great expense to our schools, would meet with a ready sale and serve a most desirable end; and we recommend the publication of such a book by said committee."

The book which we now send forth is the result of an effort to carry out this recommendation of the General Convention. As soon as the trustees had performed the previous duty of revising the Hymnal for the churches, they entered into a contract with the Christian Publishing Company, of St. Louis, by which said company assumed the financial responsibility of issuing such a book, and will pay a royalty on each book sold, which will go into the treasury of the General Convention as a mission fund.

The trustees appointed a committee of well-known brethren, in whose sound judgment and musical taste they had confidence, to select such music and words as would meet the end had in view by the Convention, and thereby greatly improve the character of the singing in our Sunday Schools. The result of their labors we now present to the brotherhood, and to the Christian public generally, hoping that it may meet with a generous reception, and succeed in filling a want that has long been felt by the Sunday Schools of the land.

Our thanks are due to the few music publishers who have generously allowed us the use of such of their pieces as we desired, free of charge. Most of the music herein contained, however, has been paid for, much of it at a high rate. We have not spared any necessary expense to make a superior book.

It is the purpose, both of the trustees and publishers, to make such gradual improvements from time to time, in the book, as may be necessary to keep it in the front line of Sunday School Hymnals. We now invoke upon the work the blessing of Him, in whose honor and for whose praise it has been prepared.

R. M. BISHOP,
Chairman Board of Trustees.

(iii)

COMPILERS' PREFACE.

THE undersigned having been charged with the responsible task of carrying out the recommendation of the General Convention, in the compilation of a Sunday School Hymnal, have spared no labor nor pains to produce such a book as would elevate the standard of Sunday School music among us, and prove of permanent value to our schools. We have steadily kept in view the character of the music and the sentiment of the words, and have endeavored, as far as possible, to rule out whatever is objectionable. Especially have we aimed to secure a class of songs that would *last*, and give our schools a long rest from the expense and inconvenience of procuring new books. We call attention to the following features of this book:

1. Each piece of music has its time-signature, or movement marks, by which the leader may determine the time in which it should be sung.

2. The words, in every case, will be found between the music staves, thus enabling the singer to see the notes and the music at the same time. This will be found of great service in learning new pieces, and also in promoting the correct singing of familiar pieces.

3. The music is written out in full, avoiding "omits," and "repeats," which are so confusing.

4. The pieces are so arranged on the pages, that no leaf need be turned in the singing of any song.

5. The department of "Songs for Special Occasions," will be found to contain a number of pieces of rare merit, adapted to a variety of special occasions.

6. While we have sought, on the one hand, to avoid light and frivolous songs, which have nothing to commend them but a merry jingle, we have aimed, on the other hand, to select nothing, which is so complex in its music, or advanced in its sentiment, as to be out of reach of children and ordinary singers.

7. The question of cost has not influenced us in the selection of songs, only as between pieces of equal merit. The publishers authorized us to get the very best songs published; and hence our selections were made *first*, and the question of cost considered afterwards.

Our work has not been done by correspondence, but by many days of united, patient labor. The Committee takes pleasure in acknowledging the very valuable services of J. P. Powell, whose labors on our Church Hymnal have been recognized and appreciated by the brotherhood. Having been appointed as musical editor of the Sunday School Hymnal, he met with us in our several meetings, and gave us the benefit of his large experience and musical taste. To him we are largely indebted for the special features of the book above mentioned. We also acknowledge, gratefully, the help received from numerous brethren, whose suggestions have aided us in ascertaining what songs have stood the test of actual service in the Sunday School.

With a vast amount of material to choose from, we have earnestly sought to make a book that would combine the best songs of the various books to which we have had access. We now send forth the result of our labors, not as a faultless book, but as one containing a larger number of excellent songs adapted to the Sunday School than any other book known to us. For it we bespeak the generous patronage of the brotherhood, and on it we implore the blessing of God, to the end that its sweet melodies and inspiring sentiments may swell the volume of praise arising from earth to heaven, and may guide many young hearts to Him, who is "the Way, the Truth, and the Life."

J. H. GARRISON.
J. H. HARDIN.
GEO. D. SITHERWOOD.

THE

CHRISTIAN SUNDAY SCHOOL HYMNAL.

No. 1. BEAUTIFUL ZION, BUILT ABOVE.

"Walk about Zion, and go round about her; tell the towers thereof."—Ps. xlviii: 12.

ANON. Metronome, ♩ = 76 = 24½ inches of string or tape. T. J. COOK.

1. Beauti-ful Zi - on, built a - bove, Beauti-ful cit - y that I love;
2. Beautiful heav'n, where all is light, Beauti-ful an - gels, clothed in white;
3. Beautiful crowns on ev - ery brow, Beauti-ful palms the conquerors show:
4. Beautiful throne for Christ our King, Beauti-ful songs the angels sing;

Beautiful gates of pearl - y white, Beauti-ful tem- ple, God its light;
Beautiful strains that nev - er tire, Beauti-ful harps through all the choir—
Beautiful robes the ransomed wear, Beauti-ful all who en - ter there—
Beautiful rest—all wanderings cease, Beauti-ful home of per - fect peace—

He who was slain on Cal -va-ry O-pens those pearl-y gates to me.
There shall I join the chorus sweet, Worshipping at the Savior's feet.
Thither I press with ea - ger feet; There shall my rest be long and sweet.
There shall my eyes the Sav-ior see; Haste to this heavenly home with me.

Refrain.

Zi - on, Zi-on, love - ly Zi - on, Beautiful Zi- on, cit- y of our God.

No. 2.

TO GOD BE THE GLORY.

"The Lord hath done great things for us, whereof we are glad!"—Ps. cxxvi: 3.

FANNY J. CROSBY.

♩ = 116 = 10½

W. H. DOANE.

1. To God be the glo - ry, great things he hath done, So loved he the
2. O per - fect re-demp-tion, the pur-chase of blood, To ev - ery be -
3. Great things he hath taught us, great things he hath done, And great our re -

S.

world that he gave us his Son, Who yield - ed his life an a -
liev - er the prom-ise of God; The vil - est of - fend - er who
joic - ing thro' Je - sus the Son; But pur - er, and high-er, and

D. S. *O come to the Fa - ther, thro'*

Fine.

tone-ment for sin, And o - pened the Life-Gate, that all may come in.
tru - ly be-lieves, Most sure-ly from Je - sus a pardon re - ceives.
great - er will be Our won-der, our trans-port, when Je- sus we see.
Je - sus the Son, And give him the glo - ry, great things he hath done.

Refrain.

Praise the Lord, praise the Lord, Let the earth hear his voice,

D. S.

Praise the Lord, praise the Lord, Let the peo - ple re - joice;

WORK FOR JESUS.

No. 3.

"Go work to-day in my vineyard."—Matt. xxi: 28.

Rev. J. H. MARTIN.   ♩ = 76 = 24½   R. M. McINTOSH.

By Permission.

1. Hear the voice of Je - sus say, Loud-ly cry - ing un - to all,
2. Why, he asks, through all the day, Stand ye i - dle, noth - ing do?
3. Work and serve me with de - light, Full re-ward to you I'll give;
4. Thro' the long and toil - some day, 'Neath a blaz- ing, burn-ing sun,

Chorus.

In my vine-yard work to-day; Hearken to his call.
En-ter in with-out de -lay: I have work for you. Work, then, for Je - sus;
At the gathering shades of night Wages you'll receive.
Bear the heat, pursue your way Till your task is done.

He will own and bless your labors, Work, work, for Je - sus: Work, work to-day.

HATFIELD.

No. 4.

"Let not your heart be troubled, neither let it be afraid."—John xiv: 27.

MARY A. S. BARBER.   ♪ = 88 = 18   W. T. PORTER.

1. Prince of peace, con - trol my will, Bid this struggling heart be still;
2. Thou hast bought me with thy blood, O - pened wide the gate of God;

Bid my fears and doubtings cease—Hush my spir- it in - to peace.
Peace I ask—but peace must be, Lord, in be - ing one with thee.

8

No. 5.

SIDNEY DYER. $\quad \bullet = 104 = 13$ LOWELL MASON.

1. Work, for the night is coming; Work thro' the morning hours; Work while the
2. Work, for the night is coming; Work thro' the sun-ny noon; Fill brightest

By permission.

dew is sparkling; Work 'mid springing flowers; Work when the day grows brighter,
hours with la-bor —Rest comes sure and soon. Give ev-ery fly-ing mo-ment

Work in the glowing sun; Work, for the night is coming, When man's work is done.
Something to keep in store; Work, for the night is coming, When man works no more.

No. 6.

DESIRE.

"For what is your life? It is even a vapor, that appeareth for a little time, and then vanisheth away."—James iv: 14

D. F. FORD. $\quad \bullet = 88 = 18$ ANON.

1. How vain is all be-neath the skies! How tran-sient ev-ery earth-ly bliss!
2. The eve-ning cloud, the morn-ing dew, The withering grass, the fad-ing flower,

How slen-der all the fond-est ties That bind us to a world like this!
Of earth-ly hopes are em-blems true—The glo-ry of a pass-ing hour.

No. 7.

"I will draw all men unto me."—John xii: 32.

Mrs. E. W. CHAPMAN.

♩ = 80 — 22

J. H. TENNEY.

By permission.

1. Clos - er to thee, my Fa-ther, draw me, I long for thine em - brace;
2. Clos - er to thee, my Sav-ior, draw me, Nor let me leave thee more,
3. Clos - er by thy sweet spirit draw me, Till I am whol - ly thine:

Clos - er with-in thine arms en-fold me, I seek a rest - ing place.
Sigh - ing to feel thine arms a-round me, And all my wanderings o'er.
Quick-en, re - fine, and wash and cleanse me, Till pure my soul shall shine.

Chorus.

Clos - er with the cords of love, Draw me to thyself a-bove;
Closer, closer with the cords of love, Draw me, draw me to thyself a - bove;

Clos - - - er draw me to thyself a-bove.
Closer with the cords of love, Draw me to thyself above, draw me to thyself a-bove.

No. 8.

TRUSTING JESUS, THAT IS ALL.

"Though he slay me, yet will I trust him."—Job xiii: 15.

EDGAR PAGE.   ♩. = 60 = 39   IRA D. SANKEY.

1. Sim - ply trust-ing ev - ery day, Trust-ing thro' a stormy way;
2. Brightly doth his spir - it shine In - to this poor heart of mine;
3. Sing - ing if my way is clear; Pray-ing if the path is drear;
4. Trust-ing him while life shall last, Trust-ing him till earth is past;

E - ven when my faith is small, Trusting Je - sus, that is all.
While he leads I can - not fall, Trusting Je - sus, that is all.
If in dan - ger, for him call; Trusting Je - sus, that is all.
Till with - in the jas - per wall, Trusting Je - sus, that is all.

Chorus.

Trust-ing as the mo-ments fly, Trust-ing as the days go by;

Trust - ing him, what-e'er be - fall, Trust-ing Je - sus, that is all.

MY PRAYER.

"Be ye therefore perfect."—Matt. 5: 48.

P. P. BLISS.　　　　　　　　　♩. = 60 = 39　　　　　　　　P. P. BLISS.

By permission.

1. More ho - li - ness give me, More striv-ings with - in;
2. More grat - i - tude give me, More trust in the Lord;
3. More pu - ri - ty give me, More strength to o'er - come;

More pa - tience in suf - fering, More sor - row for sin;
More pride in his glo - ry, More hope in his word;
More free - dom from earth - stains, More long - ings for home;

More faith in my Sav - ior, More sense of his care;
More tears for his sor - rows, More pain at his grief;
More fit for the king - dom, More use - ful I'd be;

Rit.

More joy in his serv - ice, More pur - pose in prayer.
More meek-ness in tri - al, More praise for re - lief.
More bless - ed and ho - ly, More, Sav - ior, like thee.

"And there shall be no more death, neither sorrow nor crying, neither shall there be any more pain."–Rev. xxi: 4.

Mrs. M. B. C. SLADE.   ♩—96 — 15¼   Dr. A. B. EVERETT.

By permission.

1. Be - yond this land of part - ing, los - ing, and leav - ing,
2. Be - yond this land of toil - ing, sow - ing, and reap - ing,
3. Be - yond this land of sin - ning, faint - ing, and fall - ing,
4. Be - yond this land of wait - ing, seek - ing, and sigh - ing,

Far beyond the loss - es, dark - en - ing this, And far be - yond the
Far beyond the shad - ows, dark - en - ing this, And far be - yond the
Far beyond the doubt-ings, dark - en - ing this, And far be - yond the
Far beyond the sor - rows, dark - en - ing this, And far be - yond the

tak - ing and the be - reav - ing Lies the sum -mer-land of bliss.
sigh - ing, moan - ing, and weep - ing, Lies the sum -mer-land of bliss.
griefs and dan - gers be - fall - ing, Lies the sum -mer-land of bliss.
pain, and sick - ness, and dy - ing, Lies the sum -mer-land of bliss.

Refrain.

Land be - yond,   so fair and bright! Land be-yond,   where is   no night!
Land beyond, so fair and bright!   Land beyond, where is   no night!

Summer-land,   God is its light, O   hap-py summer-land of bliss!
Summer-land,

CLOSE TO THEE.

No. 11.

"I will never leave thee nor forsake thee."—Heb. xiii: 5.

FANNY J. CROSBY.   ♩ = 88 = 18   S. J. VAIL.

By permission.

1. Thou my ev - er - last - ing por - tion, More than friend or life to me,
2. Not for ease or world-ly plea-sure, Nor for fame my prayer shall be;
3. Lead me through the vale of shad-ows, Bear me o'er life's fit - ful sea:

All a - long my pil - grim jour-ney, Sav - ior, let me walk with thee.
Glad - ly will I toil and suf - fer, On - ly let me walk with thee.
Then the gate of life e - ter - nal May I en - ter, Lord, with thee.

Refrain.

Close to thee, close to thee, Close to thee, close to thee; All a -
Close to thee, close to thee, Close to thee, close to thee; Glad - ly
Close to thee, close to thee, Close to thee, close to thee; Then the

long my pil-grim jour - ney, Sav - ior, let me walk with thee.
will I toil and suf - fer, On - ly let me walk with thee.
gate of life e - ter - nal May I en - ter, Lord, with thee.

ONCE FOR ALL.

"Justified by his grace, through the redemption that is in Christ Jesus."—Rom. iii: 24.

P. P. BLISS. ♩. = 66 = 32 P. P. BLISS.

By permission.

1. Free from the law, O hap-py con - di - tion, Je - sus hath
2. Now are we free—there's no con-dem - na - tion, Je - sus pro-
3. "Children of God," O glo - ri - ous call - ing, Sure - ly his

bled, and there is re-mis - sion : Cursed by the law and bruised by the fall,
vides a perfect sal - va - tion ; "Come un-to me," O hear his sweet call,
grace will keep us from fall - ing ; Passing from death to life at his call,

Chorus.

Grace hath redeemed us once for all.
Come, and he saves us once for all.   Once for all, O sin-ner, re-
Bless - ed sal - va - tion once for all.

ceive it, Once for all, O broth- er, be- lieve it ; Cling to the

cross, the bur-den will fall, Christ hath redeemed us once for all.

No. 13.

"The love of Christ, which passeth knowledge."—Eph. iii: 19.

CHAS. WESLEY.   ♩ = 76 = 24½   JOHN ZUNDEL.

1. Love di - vine, all love excell - ing, Joy of heaven, to earth come down,
2. Breathe, O breathe thy lov - ing Spir - it In - to ev - ery troub -led breast;

Fix in us thy hum - ble dwell-ing, All thy faith -ful mer-cies crown.
Let us all in thee in - her - it, Let us find the prom - ised rest.

Je - sus. thou art all compas-sion, Pure, unbound - ed love thou art:
Take a - way the love of sin - ning, Take our load of guilt a - way;

Vis - it us with thy sal - va - tion, En - ter ev - ery trembling heart.
End the work of thy be - gin-ning—Bring us to e - ter - nal day.

NEAR THE CROSS.

"God forbid that I should glory, save in the cross of our Lord Jesus Christ."—Gal. vi: 14.

F. C. VAN ALSTYNE.   ♩=63 =35½   W. H. DOANE.

1. Je - sus, keep me near the cross; There a pre - cious foun - tain,
2. Near the cross, a trem-bling soul, Love and mer - cy found me;
3. Near the cross! O Lamb of God, Bring its scenes be - fore me;

Free to all, a heal - ing stream, Flows from Cal -vary's moun-tain.
There the bright and morn - ing star Sheds its beams a - round me.
Help me walk from day to day, With its shad - ows o'er me.

Chorus.

In the cross, in the cross, Be my glo - ry ev - er,

Till my rap-tured soul shall find Rest be - yond the riv - er.

In "Bright Jewels."

No. 15.   "There is a friend that sticketh closer than a brother."—Prov. xviii: 24.

H. BONAR.   ♩ = 80=22   C. C. CONVERSE.

By permission.

1. What a friend we have in Je - sus, All our sins and griefs to bear!
2. Have we tri - als and tempta - tions? Is there trouble an - y-where?
3. Are we weak and heav- y - lad - en, Cumbered with a load of care?

What a priv - i - lege to car - ry Ev - ery thing to God in prayer!
We should nev - er be dis-couraged: Take it to the Lord in prayer!
Pre - cious Sav - ior, still our ref-uge—Take it to the Lord in prayer!

O what peace we oft - en for - feit, O what needless pain we bear,
Can we find a friend so faith-ful, Who will all our sorrows share?
Do thy friends de - spise, for-sake thee? Take it to the Lord in prayer;

All be - cause we do not car - ry Ev - ery thing to God in prayer!
Je - sus knows our ev - ery weakness: Take it to the Lord in prayer.
In his arms he'll take and shield thee; Thou wilt find a so-lace there.

BRINGING IN THE SHEAVES.

"He that goeth forth, bearing precious seed, shall doubtless come again with rejoicing, bringing his sheaves with him."—Ps. cxxvi: 6.

KNOWLES SHAW.

$\boldsymbol{\downarrow} = 84 = 20$

KNOWLES SHAW.

1. Sow-ing in the morn-ing, sow - ing seeds of kindness; Sow-ing in the
2. Go and tell the na - tions now in heath - en blindness;Tell them Je - sus
3. Sow-ing in the sunshine, sow - ing in the shadows; Fear-ing nei - ther

noon - tide and the dew - y eves: Wait - ing for the har - vest
died— now no ex - cuse he leaves; Bid them come to Je - sus—
clouds nor win - ter's chill - ing breeze; By and by the har - vest,

and the time of reap-ing— We shall come re - joic-ing, bring-ing in the sheaves.
thus prepare the har-vest: You shall come re - joic-ing, bring-ing in the sheaves.
and, our la - bors end - ed, We shall come re - joic-ing, bring-ing in the sheaves.

Chorus.

Bring-ing in the gold-en sheaves, Bringing in the golden
the gold-en sheaves, the

sheaves,   Wait - ing for the har- vest, and the time of   reaping—
gold - en sheaves,

We   shall   come   re - joic - ing,   bring - ing   in   the sheaves.

No. 17.   **HORTON.**

"God commendeth his love toward us, in that while we were yet sinners Christ died for us."—Rom. v: 8.

S. LONGFELLOW.   ♩ = 80 = 22   WARTENSEE.

1. Love for all! and can   it   be?   Can I   hope it   is   for me—
2. I,   the dis - o - be - dient child, Wayward, pas - sion - ate and wild;
3. I, who spurned his lov - ing hold;   I, who would not   be controlled;
4. To my Fa - ther can I   go?   At   his feet my - self I'll throw;
5. See! my Fa - ther wait - ing stands; See! he   reach - es   out his hands:

I,   who strayed so long a - go; Strayed so far, and fell so low?
I,   who left   my Fa-ther's home, In for - bid - den ways to roam;
I,   who would not hear his call;   I,   the wil - ful prod - i - gal—
.In   his house there yet may be Place—a   servant's place—for me.
God   is love; I know, I   see, Love for me—yes, e - ven me.

No. 18.

I'LL TRUST IN THEE.

"But I trusted in thee, O Lord, * * my times are in thy hands."—Ps. xxxi: 14, 15.

W. F. LLOYD. ♩. =60 =39 S. B. ELLENBERGER.

1. "My times are in thy hand;" My God, I wish them there;
2. "My times are in thy hand;" What-ev - er they may be,
3. "My times are in thy hand;" Why should I doubt or fear?
4. "My times are in thy hand;" Je - sus, the cru - ci - fied!

My life, my friends, my soul, I leave En - tire - ly to thy care.
Pleas-ing or painful, dark or bright, As best may seem to thee.
My Fa-ther's hand will nev-er cause His child a need -less tear.
The hand my cru -el sins hath pierced Is now my guard and guide.

Chorus.

"My times are in thy hand," I'll al - ways trust in thee;

I'll trust in thee, I'll trust in thee, I'll al - ways trust in thee.

By per. of Crider & Bro. York, Penna.

No. 19.   "I will guide thee with mine eye."—Ps. xxxii: 8.

NATHANIEL NILES.   ♩. = 76=24½   P. P. BLISS.

1. Pre-cious promise   God hath giv - en   To the wea - ry   passer - by,
2. When tempta-tions   almost win thee,   And thy trust-ed   watchers fly,
3. When thy se - cret hopes have perished In the grave of years gone by,
4. When the shades of life are fall - ing,   And the hour has come to die,

On the way from earth to heav - en,   "I will guide thee with mine eye."
Let this promise ring with-in   thee,   "I will guide thee with mine eye."
Let this promise still be cher-ished,   "I will guide thee with mine eye."
Hear thy trust - y   Pi - lot call - ing,   "I will guide thee with mine eye."

Refrain.

I will guide thee, I will guide thee,   I will guide thee with mine eye;

On the way from earth to heav-en,   I will guide thee with mine eye.

No. 20.   "And he, bearing his cross, went forth."—John xix: 17.

T. SHEPHERD.   ♪ = 116 = 10½   G. N. ALLEN.

1. Must Je - sus bear the cross a - lone, And all the world go free?
2. The con - se - crat - ed cross I'll bear Till death shall set me free,
3. Up - on the crys - tal pavement, down At Je - sus pierc - ed feet,
4. O pre-cious cross! O glo-rious crown! O res - ur - rec - tion day!

No; there's a cross for ev - ery one, And there's a cross for me.
And then go home my crown to wear— For there's a crown for me.
Joy-ful I'll cast my gold - en crown, And his dear name re - peat.
Ye an - gels, from the stars come down, And bear my soul a - way.

No. 21.   MY REDEEMER.

"They shall abundantly utter the memory of thy great goodness, and shall sing of thy righteousness."—Ps. cxlv: 7.

P. P. BLISS.   ♩. = 72 = 27   JAMES McGRANAHAN.

1. I will sing of my Redeem - er And his wondrous love to me;
2. I will tell the wondrous sto - ry, How my lost es - tate to save,
3. I will praise my dear Re-deem-er, His tri -umphant power I'll tell,
4. I will sing of my Re - deem-er, And his heaven-ly love to me;

On the cru - el cross he suffered, From the curse to set me free.
In his boundless love and mer - cy, He the ran - som free - ly gave.
How the vic - to - ry he giv - eth O - ver sin, and death, and hell.
He from death to life hath brought me, Son of God, with him to be.

Chorus.

Sing, O sing, ... of my Redeem - er, With his
Sing, O sing of my Redeemer, Sing, O sing of my Redeemer, With his

blood he pur - chased me, he purchased me; . . . . . . On the
blood . . . . he purchased me;
blood he pur-chased me, With his blood he purchased me;]

cross . . . . . he sealed my par - don, Paid the
cross he sealed my par-don, On the cross he sealed my pardon,

debt, and made me free, And made me free, and made me free.

24

No. 22.   THE ROCK THAT IS HIGHER.

"From the end of the earth will I cry unto thee, when my heart is overwhelmed: lead me to the rock that is higher than I."—Ps. lxi: 2.

E. JOHNSON.   ♩ = 88 = 18   W. G. FISCHER.

1. O sometimes the shadows are deep, And rough seems the path to the goal;
2. O sometimes how long seems the day, And sometimes how heavy my feet!
3. O near to the Rock let me keep, Or bless-ings or sorrows prevail;

And sor -rows, how oft-en they sweep, Like tempests, down o - ver the soul!
But, toil - ing in life's dust-y way, The Rock's blessed shadow, how sweet!
Or climbing the mountain way steep, Or walk-ing the shadow -y vale.

Chorus.

O then to the Rock let me fly,
    let me fly,   To the Rock that is

high - er than I,   O   then   to   the   Rock   let   me
is high - er than I,

fly,   To the Rock that is high - er than I.
    let me fly,

By permission.

WHEN WE WORK FOR THE LORD.

No. 23. "I can do all things through Christ, which strengtheneth me."—Phil. iv: 13.

J. H. F. ♩ = 108 = 12 J. H. FILLMORE.

1. When we work for the Lord He doth help us each day;
2. When we work for the Lord We have noth - ing to fear,
3. When we work for the Lord Ev - ery arm grow - eth strong;

He doth bless us and guide us In his own per - fect way;
For the joy of his pres - ence Bring-eth heav - en so near;
And a sweet in - spi - ra - tion Flow-eth forth in a song;

Ev - ery tri - al grows sweet, Ev - ery bur - den grows light,
While his strong arm up - holds, And we share in his love,
When the work here is done, He will take us to rest,

Rall.

And his an - gels will guard us Through the night, through the night.
We re - ceive his pro - tec - tion From a - bove, from a - bove.
We shall dwell in the man - sions Of the blest, of the blest.

By permission

WE BELIEVE.

No. 24. "Blessed are they that have not seen, and yet have believed."—John xx: 29.

A Favorite in England.   ♩ = 69=29½   KNOWLES SHAW.

1. We saw thee not when thou didst come To this poor world of sin and death;
2. We saw thee not when lift - ed high A - mid that wild and sav-age crew;
3. We gazed not in the o - pen tomb Where once thy mangled bod-y lay;
4. We walked not with the chos- en few Who saw thee from the earth as-cend;

Nor yet be-held thy cot-tage home, In that de-spis - ed Naz-a - reth;
Nor heard we that im - plor - ing cry, "Forgive, they know not what they do!"
Nor saw thee in that "up - per room," Nor met thee on the o - pen way;
Who raised to heaven their wondering view, Then low to earth all prostrate bend;

By permission.

Chorus.

But we be-lieve thy footsteps trod Its streets and plains, thou Son of God;
But we be-lieve the deed was done, That shook the earth and veiled the sun;
But we be-lieve that an - gels said, "Why seek the living with the dead?"
But we be-lieve that hu - man eyes Be-held that jour -ney to the skies;

Rit.

But we be-lieve thy foot-steps trod Its streets and plains, thou Son of God.
But we be-lieve the deed was done, That shook the earth and veiled the sun.
But we be-lieve that an - gels said, "Why seek the liv - ing with the dead?"
But we be-lieve that hu - man eyes Be-held that jour-ney to the skies.

"And Moses went up * * to the top of Pisgah, * * and the Lord showed him all the land from Gilead unto Dan."—Deut. xxxiv: 1.

SAMUEL STENNETT.   ♩=80 =22   T. C. O'KANE.

1. On Jor - dan's stormy banks I stand, And cast a wish - ful eye
2. O'er all those wide - ex - tend -ed plains Shines one e - ter - nal day;
3. When shall I reach that hap - py place, And be for - ev - er blest?
4. Filled with de - light, my rap-tured soul Would here no long - er stay;

To Ca - naan's fair and hap - py land, Where my pos - ses - sions lie.
There God, the Sun, for - ev - er reigns, And scat - ters night a - way.
When shall I see my Fa - ther's face, And in his bo - som rest?
Though Jordan's waves a - round me roll, Fear - less I'd launch a - way.

By permission.

Chorus.

We will rest in the fair and hap-py land, (by and by,) Just a - cross on the

ev - er - green shore, ... Sing the song of Mo - ses And the
ev - er - green shore,

Lamb, (by and by,) And dwell with Je - sus ev - er - more.

No. 26.

THE PEARL OF GREATEST PRICE.

"When he had found one pearl of great price, he sold all that he had and bought it."—Matt. xiii: 46.

JOHN MASON. ♩ = 84 — 20 P. P. BLISS.

By per. of John Church & Co.

1. I've found the pearl of great-est price! My heart doth sing for joy;
2. Christ is my Proph - et, Priest, and King; My Proph - et, full of light;
3. For he, in - deed, is Lord of lords, And he the King of kings;
4. Christ is my peace; he died for me, For me he shed his blood;
5. Christ Je - sus is my all in all, My com - fort and my love;

And sing I must, for Christ is mine! Christ shall my song em - ploy.
My great High Priest be - fore the throne, My King of heavenly might.
He is the Sun of righteous-ness, With heal - ing in his wings.
And, as my wondrous Sac - ri - fice, Of - fered him - self to God.
My life be - low, and he shall be My joy and crown a - bove.

Chorus.

I've found the pearl of . great-est price! My heart doth sing for joy;

And sing I must, for Christ is mine; Christ shall my song em - ploy.

No. 27. "He hath prepared for them a city."—Heb. xi: 16.

L. H. JAMESON. ♩ = 84 = 20 J. H. ROSECRANS.

1. There is a hab - i - ta - tion, Built by the liv - ing God,
2. A ci - ty with foun- da - tions Firm as th' e - ter - nal throne;
3. No night is there, no sor - row, No death and no de - cay;
4. With-in its pearl - y por - tals An - gel - ic arm - ies sing,

By permission.

For all of ev - ery na - tion, Who seek that grand a - bode.
Nor wars, nor des - o - la - tion Shall ev - er move a stone.
No yes - ter - day, no mor-row— But one e - ter - nal day.
With glo - ri - fied im - mor - tals, The prais - es of its King.

Chorus.

O Si - on, Si - on, I long thy gates to see; O
O Si - on, love - ly Si - on, O love - ly

Si - on, Si - on, When shall I dwell in thee?
Si - on, love - ly Si - on,

No. 28. I BRING MY SINS TO THEE.

"Who his own self bare our sins in his own body on the tree."—1 Pet. ii: 24.

Miss F. R. HAVERGAL. ♩=76=244½ P. P. BLISS.

1. I bring my sins to thee, The sins I can not count,
2. I bring my grief to thee, The grief I can not tell;
3. My joys to thee I bring, The joys thy love has given,
4. My life I bring to thee; I would not be my own;

That all may cleansed be In thy once o - pened fount;
No words shall need- ed be, Thou know-est all so well;
That each may be a wing To lift me near - er heaven;
O Sav - ior, let me be Thine ev - er, thine a - lone;

I bring them, Sav - ior, all to thee; The bur - den is too
I bring the sor - row laid on me, O suffering Sav - ior,
I bring them, Sav - ior, all to thee, Who hast pro-cured them
My heart, my life, my all I bring To thee, my Sa - vior

great for me, The bur - den is too great for me.
all to thee, O suf - fering Sav - ior, all to thee.
all for me, Who hast pro - cured them all for me.
and my King, To thee, my Sav - ior and my King.

THE SWEETEST NAME.

"Thou shalt call his name Jesus, for he shall save his people from their sins."—Matt. 1: 21.

NEWTON.   ♩. = 62 =35½   S. B. ELLENBERGER.

1. How sweet the name of Je - sus sounds In a be - liev-er's ear;
2. It makes the wounded spir - it whole, And calms the troubled breast;
3. Dear name, the rock on which I build, My shield and hid- ing - place;
4. I would thy boundless love pro-claim With ev - ery fleet-ing breath;

It soothes his sor - rows, heals his wounds, And drives a - way his fear.
'Tis man - na to the hun - gry soul, And to the weary rest.
My nev - er - fail-ing treas-ure, filled With boundless stores of grace.
So shall the mu - sic of thy name Re-fresh my soul in death.

Chorus.

Thy name, O Je- sus, is all my plea, Dearest and sweetest name to me;

Thou art my shield and hid-ing-place, I am re-deemed by thy rich grace.

No. 30.   "Wash me, and I shall be whiter than snow."—Ps. li: 7.

JAMES NICHOLSON.   ♩=112 — 11¼   WM. G. FISCHER.

1. Lord Je - sus, I long to be per - fect - ly whole; I
2. Lord Je - sus, look down from thy throne in the skies, And
3. Lord Je - sus, for this I most hum - bly en - treat; I
4. Lord Je - sus, thou se - est I pa - tient - ly wait; Come

want thee for - ev - er to live in my soul: Break down ev - ery
help me to make a complete sac - ri - fice: I give up my-
wait, bless- ed Lord, at thy cru - ci - fied feet; By faith, for my
now, and with - in me a new heart cre - ate. To those who have

i - dol, cast out ev - ery foe: Now wash me, and I shall be
self, and what -ev - er I know: Now wash me, and I shall be
cleansing, I see thy blood flow: Now wash me, and I shall be
sought thee, thou nev-er said'st No: Now wash me, and I shall be

Chorus.

whit - er than snow.
whit - er than snow. Whit - er than snow— yes, whit - er than
whit - er than snow.
whit - er than snow.

snow; Now wash me, and I shall be whit - er than snow.

HAPPY ZION.

No. 31. "For thy name's sake lead me and guide me."—Ps. xxxi: 3.

JAS. EDMESTON. ♩=72=27 I. B. WOODBURY.

1. Lead us, heavenly Fa - ther, lead us O'er the world's tempestuous sea;
2. Sav - ior, breathe forgive-ness o'er us: All our weakness thou dost know;
3. Let thy Spir - it, now at - tend -ing, Fill our hearts with heavenly joy;

Guard us, guide us, keep us, feed us, For we have no help but thee;
Thou didst tread this earth be - fore us, Thou didst feel its keen - est woe.
Love with ev - ery pas - sion blending, Pleas-ure that can nev - er cloy.

Yet possess - ing ev - ery bless-ing, If our God our Fa- ther be.
Lone and drea - ry, faint and wea-ry, Through the des - ert thou didst go.
Thus pro-vid - ed, pardoned, guid-ed, Noth - ing can our peace des-troy.

34

COMING NOW.

No. 32.

"Him that cometh to me, I will in nowise cast out."—John vi: 37

ROBERT MOFFETT.   ♩. = 66 = 32   FRED. A. FILLMORE.

1. Je - sus, I am com - ing now, Com - ing to the foun-tain;
2. Je - sus, make me true to thee, Pure, and meek, and low - ly,
3. Je - sus, fill my heart with peace, Flow -ing like a riv- er;

Pre - cious is th'a - ton - ing blood, Shed on Cal-vary's mountain.
While I walk the nar - row way To the cit - y ho - ly.
Day by day my joy in - crease, Till the glad for - ev - er.

Chorus.

Com - ing now, com - ing now, Seek - ing grace and fav - or,

. That my wea - ry soul may find Rest in thee for - ev - er

No. 33. "Without me ye can do nothing."—John xv: 5.

Mrs. E. P. PRENTISS. ♩= 69=29½ ROBERT LOWRY.

1. I need thee ev - ery hour, Most gra - cious Lord;
2. I need thee ev - ery hour, Stay thou near by;
3. I need thee ev - ery hour, In joy or pain;
4. I need thee ev - ery hour, Teach me thy will;
5. I need thee ev - ery hour, Most ho - ly One;

No ten - der voice like thine Can peace af - ford.
Temp - ta - tions lose their power When thou art nigh.
Come quick - ly and a - bide, Or life is vain.
And thy rich prom - i - ses In me ful - fill.
O make me thine in - deed, Thou bless - ed Son!

Refrain.

I need thee, O I need thee, Ev - ery hour I need thee;

O bless me now, my Sav - ior, I come to thee!

No. 34.   EVERY DAY.

"He exhorted them all that with purpose of heart they would cleave unto the Lord."—Acts xi: 23.

F. C. VAN ALSTYNE.   ♩ = 63 = 35½   W. H. DOANE.

1. Sav-ior, more than life to me,   I am clinging, clinging   close to thee;
2. Thro' this changing world below Lead me gent-ly,   gent-ly   as   I   go;
3. Let me love thee more and more, Till this fleeting, fleet-ing   life is o'er;

May thy rec - on- cil- ing blood Bring me nearer, near-er   still to God.
Trusting thee, I can not stray, I can nev-er,   nev -er   lose my way.
Till my soul is lost in love, In a brighter, brighter world a - bove.

Refrain.

Ev-ery day,   ev- ery hour,   Let me feel thy cleansing power;
Ev-ery day and hour, ev- ery day and hour,

May thy ten - der love to me Bind me clos-er, clos-er, Lord, to thee.

No. 36.

"Continuing instant in prayer."—Rom. xii: 12.

Mrs. M. A. KIDDER.   ♩= 88 = 18   W. O. PERKINS.

1. Ere you left your room this morn-ing Did you think to pray? In the name
2. When you met with great temp-ta - tion Did you think to pray? By his dy-
3. When your heart was filled with an - ger, Did you think to pray? Did you plead
4. When sore tri - als came up - on you, Did you think to pray? When your soul

of Christ, our Sav-ior, Did you sue for lov-ing fav - or, As a shield to-day?
ing love and mer- it, Did you claim the Ho-ly Spir-it As your guide and stay?
for grace, my brother, That you might forgive another Who had crossed your way?
was bowed in sor-row, Balm of Gil-ead did you bor-row At the gates of day?

Chorus.

O how pray-ing rests the wea-ry! Prayer will change the night to day;

So, when seems life dark and drear - y, Don't for- get to pray.

By permission.

No. 36. WHAT COULD WE DO WITHOUT JESUS.

"Lord, to whom shall we go? Thou hast the words of eternal life."—John vi: 68.

E. R. LATTA. $\bullet$. $= 66 = 32$ KNOWLES SHAW.

1. What could we do with-out Je-sus? What could the chil-dren do?
2. What could we do with-out Je-sus? What could the sin-ner do?
3. What could we do with-out Je-sus? What could the Chris-tian do?

With the long path-way be-fore them Hid-den from mor-tal view;
Where could he go for sal-va-tion? Who could his heart re-new?
Is there a friend or a broth-er E-qual-ly kind and true?

How could their foot-steps be guid-ed? Sure-ly their feet would stray,
No oth-er name has been giv-en; On-ly his blood can a-tone;
In the dark hour of temp-ta-tion, In the dread hour of pain,

But that the mer-ci-ful Sav-ior Ten-der-ly leads the way.
Sin-ners can trust but in Je-sus, Claim-ing no worth their own.
What but the mer-cy of Je-sus Can our sad hearts sus-tain?

Chorus.

What could we do with-out Je - sus? What could we do? where could we fly?

Rit.

What could we do with-out Je - sus, When we are called to die?

No. 37.　　　　　　　　**WOODWORTH.**

"Come unto me, all ye that labor and are heavy-laden, and I will give you rest."—Matt. xi: 23.

CHARLOTTE ELLIOTT.　　　$\quad \text{♩} = 88 = 18$　　　WM. B. BRADBURY.

1. Just as I am, with - out one plea, But that thy blood was shed for me,
2. Just as I am, and wait-ing not To rid my soul of one dark blot—
3. Just as I am, tho' tossed a- bout, With many a conflict, many a doubt,
4. Just as I am, poor, wretched, blind—Sight, riches, healing of the mind,

And that thou bidst me come to thee, O Lamb of God, I come, I come!
To thee, whose blood can cleanse each spot, O Lamb of God, I come, I come!
With fears with-in, and foes with-out,— O Lamb of God, I come, I come!
Yea, all I need in thee to find— O Lamb of God, I come, I come!

HE WILL HIDE ME.

No. 38. "In the shadow of his hand hath he hid me."—Isa. xlix: 2.

M. E. SERVOSS.   ♩ — 72 = 27   JAMES McGRANAHAN.

1. When the storms of life are rag-ing, Tempests wild on sea and land,
2. Though he may send some af-flic-tion, 'Twill but make me long for home;
3. En-e-mies may strive to in-jure, Sa-tan all his arts em-ploy;
4. So, while here the cross I'm bear-ing, Meet-ing storms and bil-lows wild,

I will seek a place of ref-uge In the shad-ow of God's hand.
For in love, and not in an-ger, All his chast-en-ing will come.
He will turn what seems to harm me In-to ev-er-last-ing joy.
Je-sus for my soul is car-ing; Naught can harm his Father's child.

By permission.

Chorus.

He will hide me, he will hide me, Where no harm can e'er betide me,
He will hide me, he will hide me, Where no harm can e'er betide me,

He will hide me, safe-ly hide me, In the shad-ow of his hand.
He will hide me, safely hide me, In the shadow of his hand.

No. 39.   "Jesus said unto them, Follow me."—Matt. iv: 19.

Mrs. M. B. C. SLADE.   ♩. = 66 = 32   Dr. A. B. EVERETT.

1. If I, like Gal - i - lee fish - ers, Were mend-ing my nets by the main,
2. If I were dwell-ing in plea-sure, Or sit - ting in pla-ces of gain,
3. If I were sink-ing in sad-ness, Or dreading the cross and the pain,

And Je - sus, com-ing, should call me, He nev-er should call in vain.
And Je - sus, pass - ing, should call me, He nev-er should call in vain.
And Je - sus ten - der - ly called me, He nev-er should call in vain.

By permission.

Chorus.

We'll fol-low the summons of Je - sus, Wher- ev - er, how-ev- er it falls;

When high up the pathway he sees us, And "Follow thou me!" he calls.

No. 40. THE ROCK AND THE SAND.

"Whosoever heareth these sayings of mine, and doeth them, I will liken him into a wise man, which built his house upon a rock."—Matt. vii: 24.

H. R. TRICKETT.   ♩=88—18   J. H. ROSECRANS.

1. On what are you build-ing, my brother,   Your hopes of an e - ter - nal
2. On one or the oth - er, my brother,   You're building your hopes day by
3. Your Savior has warned you, my brother,   I pray you give heed to his
4. No mat - ter how care-ful, my brother,   The sand for your house you pre-

home? It is loose, shift -ing sand, or the firm, sol - id rock, You are
day; You are risk - ing your soul on the works that you do; Will the
voice; There is life on the rock, but there's death on the sand; O my
pare, 'Twill be all swept a -way when the floods shall de-scend, Leaving

Chorus.

trust - ing for a - ges to come?
dark wa - ters sweep you a-way? Hear -ing and do - ing, we built on the rock;
broth-er, pray tell me your choice.
noth-ing but death and de-spair.

Hear-ing a - lone, we built on the sand; Both will be tried by the storm and the flood; On - ly the rock the tri - al will stand.

No. 41. **OLIVET.**

"I know whom I have believed, and am persuaded that he is able to keep that which I have committed unto him against that day."—2 Tim. i: 12.

RAY PALMER. ♩ = 88 = 18 LOWELL MASON.

1. My faith looks up to thee, Thou Lamb of Cal - va - ry,
2. May thy rich grace im - part Strength to my faint - ing heart,
3. While life's dark maze I tread, And griefs a - round me spread,
4. When ends life's tran - sient dream, When death's cold, sul - len stream

Sav - ior di - vine: Now hear me while I pray; Take all my
My zeal in - spire; As thou hast died for me, O may my
Be thou my guide; Bid dark-ness turn to day, Wipe sor-row's
Shall o'er me roll, Blest Sav - ior, then, in love, Fear and dis-

guilt a - way; O let me, from this day, Be whol - ly thine.
love to thee Pure, warm, and changeless be— A liv - ing fire.
tears a - way, Nor let me ev - er stray From thee a - side.
tress re-move; O bear me safe a - bove— A ran-somed soul.

44

PRECIOUS NAME.

No. 42.

"And blessed be his glorious name forever."—Psa. lxxii: 19.

Mrs. LYDIA BAXTER.

♩ = 104 = 13

W. H. DOANE.

1. Take the name of Je-sus with you, Child of sor-row and of woe—
2. Take the name of Je-sus ev - er, As a shield from ev- ery snare;
3. O the pre-cious name of Je-sus; How it thrills my heart with joy,
4. At the name of Je-sus bow-ing, Fall-ing prostrate at his feet,

It will joy and com- fort give you, Take it, then, where'er you go.
If temp- ta-tions round you gath- er, Breathe that ho - ly name in prayer.
When his lov - ing arms re-ceive us, And his songs our tongues employ.
King of kings in heaven we'll crown him, When our jour-ney is com-plete.

By permission.

Chorus.

Precious name, O how sweet! Hope of earth and joy of
Precious name, O how sweet!

heaven, Precious name, O how sweet—Hope of earth and joy of heaven.
Precious name, O how sweet, how sweet,

No. 43. "Christ died for our sins according to the Scriptures."—1 Cor. xv: 3.

ISAAC WATTS ♩= 116= 10½ S. J. VAIL.

1. A - las! and did my Sav - ior bleed? And did my Sove-reign die?
2. Was it for crimes that I had done He groaned up - on the tree?
3. Well might the sun in dark-ness hide, And shut his glo - ries in,
4. Thus might I hide my blushing face While his dear cross ap - pears,
5. But tears of grief can ne'er re - pay The debt of love I owe;

Would he de - vote that sa - cred head For such a worm as I?
A - maz - ing pit - y! grace un-known! And love be - yond de - gree!
When God's own Son was cru -ci - fied For man the crea-ture's sin.
Dis - solve my heart in thankful - ness, And melt mine eyes to tears.
Here, Lord, I give my - self a - way; 'Tis all that I can do.

Chorus.

Je - sus died for you, Je - sus died for me; Yes,

Je - sus died for all mankind, Bless God, sal - va - tion's free.

I LOVE TO TELL THE STORY.

No. 44.

"For I determined not to know anything among you, save Jesus Christ and him crucified."—1 Cor. ii: 2.

♩ — 100 — 14

WM. G. FISHER.

1. I love to tell the sto - ry Of un - seen things a - bove,
2. I love to tell the sto - ry, More won - der-ful it seems
3. I love to tell the sto - ry; 'Tis pleas - ant to re - peat
4. I love to tell the sto - ry: For those who know it best

Of Je - sus and his glo - ry, Of Je - sus and his love;
Than all the gold- en fan - cies Of all our gold-en dreams;
What seems, each time I tell it, More won - der - ful - ly sweet;
Seem hun - ger - ing and thirst - ing To hear it like the rest;

By permission.

I love to tell the sto - ry, Because I know 'tis true;
I love to tell the sto - ry, It did so much for me!
I love to tell the sto - ry; For some have nev - er heard
And when in scenes of glo - ry, I sing the new, new song,

It sat - is - fies my long - ings As noth - ing else can do.
And that is just the rea - son I tell it now to thee.
The mes - sage of sal - va - tion From God's own ho - ly word.
'Twill be the old, old sto - ry That I have loved so long.

Chorus.

I love to tell the sto - ry; 'Twill be my theme in glo- ry,

To tell the old, old sto - ry Of Je - sus and his love.

No. 45.   **HOUR OF PARTING.**

"Thou shalt guide me with thy counsel, and afterward receive me to glory."—Psalms lxxiii: 24.

Dr. T. G. CHATTLE.   ♩. = 60 = 30   WM. W. BENTLEY.

By permission.

1. Gen- tle Sav - ior, be thou near us,   As we from each oth- er part;
2. As the clos - ing hour draws near us, And the night steals gently on,
3. When the night of death comes o'er us, And our earth-ly prayers are o'er,

May thy word, its truth im-press-ing, Shed its light on ev - ery heart.
Let thy gra-cious presence cheer us, Guard us till the com-ing morn.
O re - ceive us home to glo - ry, There to praise thee ev - er- more.

No. 46.

THE GATE AJAR FOR ME.

"The gates of it shall not be shut at all by day; for there shall be no night there."—Rev. xxi: 25.

Mrs. LYDIA BAXTER. $\quad \textit{d.} = 63 = 35\frac{1}{2}$ PHILIP PHILLIPS.

1. There is a gate that stands a - jar, And thro' its por - tals gleam-ing,
2. That gate a - jar stands free for all Who seek through it sal - va - tion;
3. Press onward, then, though foes may frown, While mercy's gate is o - pen,
4. Beyond the riv - er's brink we'll lay The cross that here is giv - en,

A ra - diance from the cross a - far The Sav-ior's love re - veal - ing.
The rich and poor, the great and small, Of ev - ery tribe and na - tion.
Ac-cept the cross and win the crown, Love's ev - er - last - ing tok - en.
And bear the crown of life a - way, And love him more in heav - en.

By permission.

Refrain.

O depths of mer - cy! can it be That gate was left a - jar for me?

For me, . . . for me, . . . Was left a - jar for me?
For me, for me,

"There is none other name under heaven given among men whereby we must be saved."—Acts iv: 12.

ANON.   ♩ = 84 = 20   J. D. TRAPP.

1. Let the ho - ly name of Je - sus Dwell for- ev - er in thy heart;
2. Souls all wea-ry, worn, and troub-led, Bowed with sorrow, pain, and grief;

It will cleanse, re -fresh, and cheer you, Shield from Satan's fa - tal dart.
Weak and trembling—in this fountain Sure - ly find a sweet re- lief.

O the joy, the pre- cious fountain. Which his sa - cred name supplies;
With thy woes and earth - ly la - bors, Wea - ry with thy load of care;

It is balm for wounded spir-its, It is life that nev - er dies.
Come, O come un - to the Sav-ior, In him end-less pleasures are.

I WANT TO BE LIKE JESUS.

No. 48.

"Who loved me and gave himself for me."—Gal. ii: 20.

A. K. MILLER.

♩ = 76 = 244

FRANK M. DAVIS.

1. I want to be like Je - sus, So low - ly and so meek;
2. I want to be like Je - sus, So fre - quent - ly in prayer;
3. I want to be like Je - sus, En-gaged in do - ing good,
4. A - las! I'm not like Je - sus, As a - ny one may see;

For no one marked an an - gry word That ev - er heard him speak.
A - lone up - on the mountain top, He met his Fa - ther there.
So that of me it may be said, He hath done what he could.
Thy gen - tle Spir - it, Sav - ior, send, And make me like to thee.

By permission.

Chorus.

I want to be like Je - sus, God's well- be - lov - ed Son;

I want to be like Je - sus, The pure and ho - ly One.

No. 49.

"Who shall separate us from the love of Christ?"—Rom. viii: 35.

Mrs. EMILY H. MILLER.   ♩ = 80 = 22   GEO. F. ROOT.

1. I love to hear the sto - ry Which an - gel voi - ces tell,
2. I'm glad my bless - ed Sav - ior Was once a child like me,
3. To sing his love and mer - cy, My sweet - est songs I'll raise,

How once the King of glo - ry Came down on earth to dwell;
To show how pure and ho - ly His lit - tle ones might be;
And though I can not see him, I know he hears my praise;

I am both weak and sin - ful, But this I sure - ly know,
And if I try to fol - low His foot - steps here be - low,
For he has kind - ly prom - ised That I shall sure - ly go

The Lord came down to save me, Be - cause he loved me so.
He nev - er will for - get me, Be - cause he loves me so.
To sing a - mong his an - gels, Be - cause he loves me so.

No. 50.

THE LAMBS OF THE UPPER FOLD.

"He shall gather the lambs with his arm, and carry them in his bosom."—Isa. xl: 11.

PAULINA. $\quad = 92 = 16\frac{1}{2}$ Rev. B. R. HANBY.

1. 'Mid the pas - tures green of the bless - ed isles, Where
2. There are ti - ny mounds where the hopes of earth Were

nev - er is heat or cold, Where the light of life is the
laid 'neath the tear - wet mold, But the light that paled at the

Shepherd's smile, Are the lambs of the up - per fold. Where the
strick - en hearth Was joy to the up - per fold. O the

lil - ies blos-som in fade - less spring, And nev- er a heart grows
white stone bear -eth a new name now, That nev-er on earth was

By permission.

old, Where the glad new song is the song they sing,
told, And the ten - der Shep · herd doth guard with care

Are the lambs of the up - per fold. Lambs of the up - per
The lambs of the up - per fold. Lambs of the up - per

fold, Lambs of the up - per fold, Where the glad new song
fold, Lambs of the up - per fold, And the ten - der Shep -

is the song they sing, Are the lambs of the up - per fold.
herd doth guard with care The lambs of the up - per fold.

No. 51.   "We shall be like him."—1 John iii: 2.

W. J. K.   ♩ = 76 = 24½   W. J. KIRKPATRICK.

1. Je - sus, Sa- vior, great Ex - am - ple, Pat- tern of all pur - i - ty,
2. Lest I wan- der from thy pathway, Or my feet move wea - ri - ly,
3. When temp-ta- tions fiercely low- er, And my shrinking soul would flee,
4. When a - round me all is darkness, And thy beau-ties none may see,
5. When death's cold and chilling fin-ger Leaves its impress on my brow,

I would fol - low in thy footsteps, Dai - ly growing more like thee.
Sav - ior, take my hand and lead me, Keep me steadfast : more like thee.
Change each weakness in - to pow- er, Keep me spotless : more like thee.
May thy beams, O Glorious Brightness, In ef-ful-gence shine through me.
May thy life, with- in me swell-ing, Keep me sing-ing then as now.

By permission.

Chorus.

More like thee,   more like thee;   Savior, this my constant prayer shall
More like thee,   more like thee;

be—Day by day, wher-e'er I stay, Make me more and more like thee.

No. 52. "I the Lord have called thee."—Isa. xlii: 6.

Mrs. S. A. COLLINS. $\quad = 60 = 39$ W. H. DOANE.

1. Je - sus, gra-cious one,call - eth now to thee, "Come,O sinner, come!"
2. Still he waits for thee,pleading pa - tient- ly, "Come,O come to me!
3. Wea-ry, sin - sick soul,called so gra - cious - ly,Canst thou dare re - fuse?

Calls so ten-der - ly, calls so lov - ing - ly, "Now,O sin - ner, come."
Heav - y - lad -en one, I thy grief have borne,Come and rest in me."
Mer - cy of-fered thee,free - ly, ten - der - ly, Wilt thou still a - buse?

Refrain.

Words of peace and blessing,Christ's own love confessing;
Words of love o'er-flowing, Life and bliss be-stow-ing; Hear the sweet voice of
Come, for time is fly - ing,Haste,thy lamp is dy - ing;

Jesus,Full,full of love ;Calling tenderly,calling lovingly,"Come,O sinner,come."

No. 53. **WHO'S ON THE LORD'S SIDE?**

"And Moses stood in the gate of the camp, and said, Who is on the Lord's side?"—Ex. xxxii: 26.

PAULINA. ♩ = 100 = 14 P. P. B.

1. We're marching to Ca - naan with ban-ner and song, We're sol-diers en-
2. The sword may be burnished, the arm- or be bright, For Sa - tan ap-
3. Who is there a-mong us yet un- der the rod, Who knows not the
4. O, heed not the sor - row, the pain and the wrong, For soon shall our

list - ed to fight 'gainst the wrong; But, lest in the con - flict our
pears as an an - gel of light; Yet dark - ly the bo - som may
par - don - ing mer - cy of God? O, bring to him hum-bly the
sigh - ing be changed in - to song? So, bear - ing the cross of our

strength should divide, We ask, Who a-mong us is on the Lord's side?
treach - er - y hide, While lips are pro-fess - ing, "I'm on the Lord's side."
heart in its pride; O, haste while he's wait-ing and seek the Lord's side.
cov - e-nant Guide, We'll shout, as we tri-umph, "I'm on the Lord's side!"

Chorus.

O, who is there a-mong us, the true and the tried, Who'll stand by his col - ors—who's on the Lord's side? O, who is there a - mong us, the

true and the tried, Who'll stand by his col - ors—who's on the Lord's side?

No. 54.   **YARBROUGH.**

"He died for all that they which live should not henceforth live unto themselves, but unto him which died for them and rose again."—2 Cor. v: 15.

Miss FRANCES E. HAVERGAL.   ♩ = 66 = 32   Arr. by R. M. McINTOSH.

1. Take my life, and   let it   be   Con - se - cra - ted, Lord, to   thee;
2. Take my feet, and   let them   be   Swift and beau - ti - ful for   thee;
3. Take my sil - ver   and my   gold, Not a   mite would   I with - hold;
4. Take my will and make it   thine, It shall be   no   long - er   mine;
5. Take my love; my Lord, I   pour   At thy   feet   its   treas-ure - store;

CHO.—Lord, I give my life to thee, Thine for - ev - er - more to be,

Take my hands, and   let them move   At the im - pulse of thy   love.
Take my voice, and   let me   sing   Al-ways, on - ly   for my King.
Take my mo - ments and my days, Let them flow in ceaseless praise.
Take my heart, it   is thine own, It shall be   thy roy - al throne.
Take my-self, and   I will   be   Ev - er, on - ly,   all for   thee.

Lord, I give my life to thee, Thine for - ev - er - more to be.

58

PRECIOUS WORDS.

No. 55. "The gospel is the power of God unto salvation."—Rom. 1: 16.

Mrs. LOULA K. ROGERS.   ♩. = 69 = 29½   R. M. McINTOSH.

1. Pre-cious for - ev - er! O won - der - ful words, Teach me the
2. Free - ly he of - fers their prom- ise to all, "Come un - to
3. Wouldst thou refuse the sweet sol - ace he gives In the mid-

pathway of du - ty; Lead me be - side the still wa - ters of life,
me who -so - ev - er;" Sin - ners oppressed with a bur - den of woe,
night of thy sor-row? Wouldst thou go on in the darkness of sin,

Refrain.

Flow -ing through val - leys of beau-ty.
Drink of the boun - ti - ful riv -er.   Precious for - ev - er to
Long- ing for no bright to - morrow?

you and to me, Words that our Sav - ior has spok-en, Bear - ing sal -

By permission of R. M. McINTOSH.

va-tion far o - ver the sea, Heal - ing the hearts that are brok - en!

MORE LOVE.

No. 56.

"Lovest thou me?"—John xxi: 16.

E. P. PRENTISS.

♩=100＝14

T. E. PERKINS.

By permission.

1. More love to thee, O Christ! More love to thee! Hear thou the
2. Once earth-ly joy I craved—Sought peace and rest; Now thee a -
3. Then shall my lat - est breath Whis - per thy praise; This be the

prayer I make, On bend - ed knee; This is my earn - est plea—
lone I seek: Give what is best. This all my prayer shall be—
part - ing cry My heart shall raise— This still its prayer shall be,

More love, O Christ, to thee! More love, O Christ, to thee, More love to thee!

OVER THERE.

No. 57. "Glorious things are spoken of thee, O city of God." T. C. O'KANE.

ANON.

♩ = 96 = 15¼

1. O think of a home o-ver there, By the side of the riv-er of
2. O think of the friends o-ver there, Who be-fore us the jour-ney have
3. My Sav-ior is now o-ver there, There my kin-dred and friends are at
4. I'll soon be at home o-ver there, For the end of my jour-ney I

light, o-ver there, Where the saints, all im-mor-tal and fair, Are
trod, o-ver there, Of the songs that they breathe on the air, In their
rest, o-ver there, Then a-way from my sor-row and care Let me
see, o-ver there, Man-y dear to my heart o-ver there, Are

Refrain.

robed in their garments of white, o-ver there. O-ver there, o-ver there,
home in the pal-ace of God, o-ver there. O-ver there, o-ver there,
fly to the land of the blest, o-ver there. O-ver there, o-ver there,
watching and wait-ing for me, o-ver there. O-ver there, o-ver there,

o-ver there, o-ver there, O think of the home o-ver there, o-ver there,
o-ver there, o-ver there, O think of the friends o-ver there, o-ver there,
o-ver there, o-ver there, My Sav-ior is now o-ver there, o-ver there,
o-ver there, o-ver there, I'll soon be at home o-ver there, o-ver there,

By permission.

Over there, over there, over there, over there, O think of a home o - ver there.
Over there, etc.
Over there, etc.
Over there, etc.

WHAT HAST THOU DONE FOR ME?

No. 58.　"So Christ was once offered to bear the sins of many."—Heb. ix: 28.

Miss F. R. HAVERGAL.　　　$\quad = 63 = 35\frac{1}{2}$　　　P. P. BLISS.

By permission.

1. I　gave　my life　for　thee,　My pre - cious blood　I　shed,
2. My　Fa - ther's house　of　light—　My glo - ry - cir - cled throne,
3. I　suf - fered much for　thee,　More than thy tongue can　tell,
4. And I have brought to　thee,　Down from my home　a - bove,

That thou might'st ransomed　be,　And quick-ened from the　dead;
I　left　for earth - ly　night,　For wanderings sad and　lone;
Of　bit - terest ag - o -　ny,　To res - cue thee from　hell;
Sal - va - tion full and　free,　My par - don and my　love;

I　gave, I　gave my　life for thee, What hast thou given for　me?
I　left, I　left it　all for thee, Hast thou left aught for　me?
I've borne, I've borne it　all for thee, What hast thou borne for　me?
I　bring, I　bring rich gifts to thee, What hast thou brought to　me?

62

LOVE OF JESUS.

No. 59.

"Having loved his own * * * he loved them unto the end."—John xiii: 1.

♩ = 100 = 14

T. E. PERKINS.

1. There is no love like the love of Je - sus, Nev-er to fade or fall,
2. There is no heart like the heart of Je - sus, Filled with a ten- der love;
3. O let us hark to the voice of Je - sus, O may we nev-er roam,

Till in - to the fold of the peace of God He has gath-ered us all.
No throb nor throe that our hearts can know, But he feels it a-bove.
Till safe we rest on his lov - ing breast, In the dear heavenly home.

By permission.

Chorus.

Je - sus' love, pre-cious love, Bound-less, and pure, and free; O

turn to that love, wea - ry, wandering soul, Je - sus pleadeth for thee.

No. 60.

"For if we believe that Jesus died and rose again, even so them also which sleep in Jesus, will God bring with him."—1 Thess. iv: 14.

W. T. D. $\quad \ =72=27$ Arr. from W. T. DALE.

1. O - ver Jor - dan we shall meet, By and by, by and ly,
2. All our sor - rows shall be past, By and by, by and by;
3. There we'll join the ran-somed throng, By and by, by and by,

In a fel - low - ship so sweet, By and by, by and by;
We shall reach our home at last, By and by, by and by;
Chant - ing love's re - deem - ing song, By and by, by and by;

We shall gath - er on the shore, With our kin - dred gone be - fore,
With the ran- somed we shall stand There, a ho - ly, hap - py band,
There we'll meet be - fore the throne, There we'll lay our tro-phies down,

And the Sav - ior's name a - dore, By and by, by and by.
Crowned with glo - ry in that land, By and by, by and by.
And re - ceive a shin - ing crown, By and by, by and by.

by permission.

IS MY NAME WRITTEN THERE?

No. 61.

"Rejoice, because your names are written in heaven."—Luke x: 20.

W. T. G.

♩—108 = 12

W. T. GIFFE.

1. In the Lamb's book of life, that is kept in heav - en, Are
2. All the good that I do is there re - cord - ed, And in
3. Though my life may be fraught with af - flic - tions fear - ful, I can

writ - ten the names of those for - giv - en; Is my name writ-ten there?
heav- en by grace I'll be re - ward-ed: Is my name writ-ten there?
bear with it all, and my heart be cheer-ful, If my name's writ-ten there.

Chorus.

Is my name writ - ten there? Is my name writ - ten there?

In the Lamb's book of life, Is my name writ - ten there?

FOUNTAIN.

"In that day there shall be a fountain opened to the house of David for sin and for uncleanness."—Zech. xiii: 1.

WM. COWPER. ♩ = =22 American Melody.

1. There is a foun-tain filled with blood, Drawn from Im-man - uel's veins;
2. The dy - ing thief rejoiced to see That foun- tain in his day:
3. O Lamb of God, thy precious blood Shall nev - er lose its power,
4. E'er since by faith I saw the stream Thy flow- ing wounds sup - ply,
5. And when this lisp-ing,stam'ring tongue Lies si - lent in the grave,

And sinners, plunged be- neath that flood, Lose all their guilt - y stains,
And there have I, as vile as he, Washed all my sins a - way,
Till all the ransomed Church of God Be saved, to sin no more,
Re - deem-ing love has been my theme, And shall be till I die,
Then, in a no - bler, sweet-er song I'll sing thy power to save,

Lose all their guilt - y stains, Lose all their guilt - y stains;
Washed all my sins a - way, Washed all my sins a - way;
Be saved, to sin no more, Be saved, to sin no more;
And shall be till I die, And shall be till I die;
I'll sing thy power to save, I'll sing thy power to save;

And sinners, plunged be-neath that flood, Lose all their guilt - y stains.
And there have I, as vile as he, Washed all my sins a - way.
Till all the ransomed Church of God Be saved, to sin no more.
Re - deem-ing love has been my theme, And shall be till I die.
Then, in a no - bler, sweeter song, I'll sing thy power to save.

No. 63.

O THE DEBT OF LOVE.

"For his great love wherewith he loved us."—Eph. ii: 4.

EDW. J. ARMSTRONG.

$\quad = 76 = 24\frac{1}{2}$

W. F. SHERWIN.

All my life the Lord hath led me; All my life his lov - ing care
O how ten - der - ly he brought me O'er the toil-some, dangerous way;
As I am, O Sav - ior, take me! Though a sin - ner, save me, Lord!

'Midst the wild -er - ness hath fed me; Still his hands my ways pre - pare.
With his own dear blood he bought me; How can I his love re - pay?
Cleanse my soul from sin, and make me Pure in spir - it by thy word.

By permission.

Refrain.

O the debt of love I owe him, Debt no gold can e'er re - pay;

If I can but see and know him, He my sin will wash a - way.

WONDERFUL WORDS OF LIFE.

"The words that I speak unto you, they are spirit, they are life."—John vi: 63.

P. P. B. $\quad \cdot = 63 = 35\frac{1}{2}$ P. P. BLISS.

By permission.

1. Sing them o - ver a - gain to me, Won-der - ful words of Life;
2. Christ, the bless - ed One, gives to all Won-der - ful words of Life;
3. Sweet- ly ech - o the gos - pel call, Won-der - ful words of Life;

Let me more of their beauty see, Won-der-ful words of Life. Words of life and
Sin-ner, list to the lov-ing call, Won-der-ful words of Life. All so free-ly
Of - fer par-don and peace to all, Won-der-ful words of Life. Je-sus, on- ly

Refrain.

beau - ty, Teach me faith and du - ty,
giv - en, Woo - ing us to heav - en, Beau - ti - ful words, wonder-ful words,
Sav - ior, Sanc - ti - fy for - ev - er.

Wonderful words of Life, Beautiful words, wonderful words, Wonderful words of Life.

HEAR HIM CALLING.

No. 65.

"I am the good Shepherd."—John x: 11.

Mrs. M. B. C. SLADE.

$\stackrel{.}{\downarrow} = 96 = 15\frac{1}{4}$

Dr. A. BROOKS EVERETT.

By permission.

1. Are you stay - ing, safe - ly stay - ing, In the ten - der
2. Are you hear - ing, glad - ly hear - ing, How he bids his
3. Are you roam - ing, long - er roam - ing, In the cold, dark

Shepherd's peaceful fold? No, I'm stray - ing, sad - ly straying, On the
fold - ed flock re-joice? No, I'm fear - ing, sad - ly fear - ing, I have
night of doubt and sin? No, I'm com - ing, quick-ly com-ing! O - pen

Refrain.

lone - ly mountains, dark and cold.
fol - lowed far the stranger's voice. On your ear his lov - ing tones are
door! make haste to let me in!

fall - ing, For he seeks you, where - so - e'er you roam, Hear him, call - ing, sweet-ly call - ing, As he bids his wandering sheep come home.

No. 66. **BOOK OF LIFE.**

"All scripture is given by inspiration of God, and is profitable for doctrine, for reproof, for correction, for instruction in righteousness."—2 Tim. iii: 16.

ANON. $\quad = 93 = 16\frac{1}{2}$ Dr. L. MASON.

By permission.

1. Book of grace, and book of glo - ry! Gift of God to age and youth;
2. Book of love! in ac - cents ten - der, Speak-ing un - to such as we;
3. Book of hope! the spir - it, sigh - ing, Con - so - la - tion finds in thee,
4. Book of life! when we, re - pos - ing, Bid fare-well to friends we love,

Wond - rous in thy sa - cred sto - ry, Bright, bright with truth,
May it lead us, Lord, to ren - der All, all to thee,
As it hears the Sav - ior cry - ing— "Come, come to me,"
Give us for the life then clos - ing, Life, life a - bove,

Wond - rous in thy sa - cred sto - ry, Bright, bright with truth.
May it lead us, Lord, to ren - der All, all to thee.
As it hears the Sav - ior cry - ing—"Come, come to me."
Give us for the life then clos - ing, Life, life a - bove.

No. 67.

MERCY.

"I'll sing of the mercies of the Lord forever."—Psalms, lxxxix: 1.

FANNY CROSBY.   ♩ = 72 = 27   WM. B. BRADBURY.

By permission.

1. I'll sing the glo - ry of the Lord, His good - ness I'll pro-claim,
2. I'll sing of Christ, the Ho - ly One, Who bore the cross for me;
3. I'll sing the mer - cy of the Lord, And praise him while I've breath;

And tell how great his mer- cies are To those that fear his name;
His all a - ton - ing sac - ri - fice My pre - cious theme shall be,
I'll trust in him whose rod and staff Will com - fort me in death.

Up to the ev - er - last - ing hills I'll lift my wait- ing eyes,
High on his throne ex - alt - ed now He sits at God's right hand;
Dis - solve, O earth - ly house of clay, And let my spir - it soar,

And there, with ear- ly morning light, My grate - ful prayer shall rise,
The on - ly ref- uge of my soul, The rock on which I stand,
With all the ransomed hosts a-bove, To praise him ev - er-more,

And there, with ear - ly morning light,
The on - ly ref - uge of my soul,
With all the ran - somed hosts a - bove,

And there, with ear-ly morning light,
The on-ly ref-uge of my soul,
With all the ransomed hosts a-bove,

My grate-ful prayer shall rise.
The rock on which I stand.
To praise him ev-er-more.

And there, with ear - ly　morning light,
The　on - ly ref - uge　of my soul,
With　all the ran - somed　hosts a - bove,

No. 68.　　　SOMETHING FOR JESUS.
"Who loved me and gave himself for me."—Gal. ii: 20.

S. D. PHELPS.　　　　♩ = 96 = 15¼　　　　ROBERT LOWRY.

1. Sav - ior, thy dy - ing love　Thou gav - est　me;　Nor should I
2. O'er the blest mer - cy-seat,　Pleading for me,　My fee - ble
3. Give me a faith-ful heart—　Likeness to thee—　That each de-

aught withhold, Dear Lord, from thee. In love my soul would bow, My heart ful-
faith looks up, Je - sus. to thee. Help me the cross to bear, Thy wondrous
part-ing day, Henceforth may see Some work of love be-gun, Some deed of

fill its vow, Some of-fering bring thee now, Some-thing for thee.
love de-clare, Some song to raise, or pray'r; Some-thing for thee.
kind-ness done, Some wanderer sought and won,— Some-thing for thee.

No. 69.

I'M REDEEMED.

"Behold the Lamb of God."—John 1: 29.

T. C. O'K.   ♩=100=14   T. C. O'KANE.

1. O sing of   Je - sus, "Lamb of God," Who died on Cal - va - ry,
2. O wondrous power of   love di - vine! So pure, so full, so free!
3. All glo - ry now to Christ the Lord, And ev - er-more shall be;

And for   a   ran - som shed his blood, For you and e - ven me.
It reach - es   out   to all man-kind, Em - brac - es   e - ven me.
He hath redeemed a world from sin, And ransomed e - ven me.

By permission.

Refrain.

I'm re - deemed,   I'm   re - deemed,   Through the
I'm redeemed,   I'm redeemed, Through the

blood of the Lamb that was slain, . . . I'm re - deemed,
blood of the Lamb, of the Lamb that was slain,   I'm redeemed,

I'm re - deemed, Hal - le - lu - jah un - to his name.
I'm redeemed,

No. 70. **PURER IN HEART.**

"Blessed are the pure in heart, for they shall see God."—Matt. v: 8.

Mrs. A. L. DAVISON. ♩ = 100 = 14 J. H. FILLMORE.

By permission

1. Pur - er in heart, O God, Help me to be; May I de
2. Pur - er in heart, O God, Help me to be; Teach me to
3. Pur - er in heart, O God, Help me to be; That I thy

vote my life Whol - ly to thee. Watch thou my way - ward feet,
do thy will Most lov - ing - ly. Be thou my Friend and Guide,
ho - ly face One day may see. Keep me from se - cret sin,

Guide me with coun - sel sweet; Pur - er in heart Help me to be.
Let me with thee a - bide; Pur - er in heart Help me to be.
Reign thou my soul with - in; Pur - er in heart Help me to be.

74

No. 71.

WHERE HE LEADS WE WILL FOLLOW.

"He leadeth me beside the still waters."—Ps. xxiii: 2.

P. P. BLISS.

♩ = 72 = 27

P. P. BLISS.

1. See the gen - tle Shepherd stand-ing Where the qui - et wa-ters flow;
2. On - ly by the door we en - ter; All who en - ter he will save;
3. Safe within the fold he leads us, He the Shepherd, we his own;

To the pas - tures green in - vit - ing, Hun - gry, thirst - y, let us go.
Life a - bundant - ly be - stow -ing, Though his life the Shepherd gave.
And as him the Fa - ther know-eth, Precious thought-of him we're known.

by permission.

Chorus.

Where he leads we will fol-low, Where he leads we will fol-low,

Where he leads we will fol - low, We will fol -low all the way.

No. 72.

"If any man will come after me, let him deny himself, and take up his cross and follow me."—Matt. xvi: 24.

M. B. SLEIGHT.   ♩ = 80 = 22   H. R. PALMER.

1. Hark! the voice of Je - sus call - ing, "Fol - low me, fol - low me!"·
2. Who will heed the ho - ly man-date, "Fol - low me, fol - low me?"
3. Heark - en, lest he plead no long - er, "Fol - low me, fol - low me!"

Soft - ly through the si - lence fall - ing, "Fol - low, fol - low me!"
Leav - ing all things at his bid-ding, "Fol - low, fol - low me!"
Once a - gain, O hear him call - ing, "Fol - low, fol - low me!"

As of old he called the fish - ers, When he walked by Gal - i - lee,
Hark! that ten - der voice en - treat - ing Mar - i - ners on life's rough sea,
Turn - ing swift at thy sweet summons, Ev - er - more, O Christ, would we,

Rit.

Still his pa - tient voice is plead-ing, "Fol - low, fol - low me!"
Gent - ly, lov - ing - ly re - peat - ing, "Fol - low, fol - low me!"
For thy love all else for - sak - ing, Fol - low, fol - low thee!

No. 73.

WHAT SHALL THE HARVEST BE?

"Whatsoever a man soweth, that shall he also reap."—Gal. vi: 7.

ANON.

$\quad = 60 = 39$

P. P. BLISS.

1. Sow - ing the seed by the day - light fair, Sow - ing the seed by the noon-day glare, Sow - ing the seed in the sol - emn night; O what shall the har-vest be? O what shall the har-vest be?

2. Sow - ing the seed by the way - side high, Sow - ing the seed on the rocks to die, Sow - ing the seed in the fer - tile soil; O what shall the har-vest be? O what shall the har-vest be?

3. Sow - ing the seed of a ling-ering pain, Sow - ing the seed of a maddened brain, Sow - ing the seed of e - ter - nal shame; O what shall the har-vest be? O what shall the har-vest be?

4. Sow - ing the seed with an ach - ing heart, Sow - ing the seed while the tear-drops start, Glad - ly to gath -er the har - vest home; O what shall the har-vest be? O what shall the har-vest be?

By permission.

Chorus.

Sown . . . . in the dark - - - ness or sown . . . . in the

Sown in the darkness or sown in the light,   Sown in the darkness or

light, . . .   Sown . . . . in our weak - - - - - ness or

sown in the light, Sown in our weakness or sown in our might,

sown . . . . in our might, . . .   Gath - ered in time or e-

Sown in our weakness or sown in our might, Gath - ered in time or e-

ter - - ni - ty, Sure,   ah, sure will the har - vest be.

ter - ni - - ty, Sure, ah,   sure will the   har - - vest, harvest be.

PRAISE THE LORD.

No. 74.

"It is good to sing praises unto our God."—Ps. cxlvii: 1.

Mrs. M. B. C. SLADE. $\quad \bullet = 104 = 13$ Dr. A. B. EVERETT.

1. Praise the Lord! (praise the Lord!) praise the Lord! (praise the Lord!) Hap-py
2. Love the Lord! (love the Lord!) love the Lord! (love the Lord!) Hap-py
3. Serve the Lord! (serve the Lord!) serve the Lord! (serve the Lord!) Hap-py

chil - dren now in the tem - ple sing, Praise the Lord! (praise the Lord!)
chil - dren, give him your youth's bright days; Love the Lord! (love the Lord!)
chil - dren, serve him with songs of joy; Serve the Lord! (serve the Lord!)

praise the Lord! Ho - san - na to the Lord our King. O praise him for the
love the Lord! He ev - er lov- eth you, he says. O love him, for he
serve the Lord! And let his work your hands employ. O serve him, what-so-

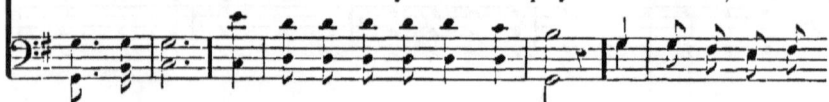

flowers that grow, O praise him for the stars that move; Praise the
loves us so; O love him for his won-drous love; Love the
e'er ye do; O serve him where -so - e'er ye move; Serve the

Lord(praise the Lord)here be-low,   And praise him in   his courts a - bove.
Lord(love the Lord)here be-low,   And love him in   his courts a - bove.
Lord(serve the Lord)here be-low,   And serve him in   his courts a - bove.

No. 75.   **EVEN ME.**

"Bless me, even me, also, O my Father!"—Gen. xxvii: 34

CODNER. $\cdot = 58 = 42$ T. E. PERKINS.

By permission.

1. Lord, I hear of showers of blessings Thou art scattering full and free;
2. Pass me not, O God, our Fa-ther! Sin - ful though my heart may be;
3. Pass me not, O gra-cious Sav- ior? Let me live and cling to thee!
4. Love of God—so pure and changeless; Blood of Christ—so rich, so free;

Showers the thirst - y land re-fresh -ing, Let some droppings fall on me;
Thou might'st leave me, but the rath- er Let thy mer- cy fall on me;
For I'm long - ing for thy fav - or; While thou'rt calling,call on me;
Grace of God— so strong and boundless, Mag -ni - fy it all in me;

E - ven me, e - ven me! Let some droppings fall on me.
E - ven me, e - ven me! Let thy mer - cy fall on me.
E - ven me, e - ven me! While thou'rt call - ing, call on me.
E - ven me, e - ven me! Mag-ni - fy it all in me.

80

No. 76.

WHERE'ER THOU GOEST.

"Whither thou goest I will go."—Ruth i: 16.

T. E. HALL. ♩ = 58 = 42 T. E. HALL.

1. Where'er thou go - est I will go: Dear Sav - ior, lead the way;
2. Where'er thou go - est I will go, Though up the mountain steep;
3. Where'er thou go - est I will go, Though in some lone- ly dell;
4. Where'er thou go - est I will go, Through all my life's rough way;

Just where, or how, I do not know, But thou'lt not lead a - stray.
A faith - ful Guide thou art, I know, So close to thee I'll keep.
Thou wilt be there—how sweet to know, And cheer-less hours dis - pel.
And, at its end, I'll pass, I know, In - to an end - less day.

Chorus.

Wher - e'er thou go - est I will go, Near thee I'll keep each day;

Where'er thou go - est I will go, Through all life's wea - ry way.

Copyright, 1879, by Asa Hall.

No. 77.   "Casting all your care upon him, for he careth for you."—1 Peter v: 7.

Mrs. M. A. W. COOK.   ♩ = 108 = 12

By permission.

1. In some way or oth - er   the Lord will   pro- vide: It may not   be
2. At some time or oth - er   the Lord will   pro- vide: It may not   be
3. Despond, then, no long - er,   the Lord will   pro- vide;   And this   be   the
4. March on, then, right bold-ly;   the sea shall   di - vide;   The path-way   made

my way,   It may not   be   thy way; And   yet,   in   his   own way,   "The
my time,   It may not   be   thy time; And   yet,   in   his   own time,   "The
to - ken— No word he hath spo-ken   Was   ev - er   yet   bro- ken: "The
glo- rious, With shoutings vic - to- rious,   We'll join   in   the   cho- rus,   "The

Chorus.

Lord will pro- vide."
Lord will pro- vide."   Then we'll trust   in   the Lord,   And   he   will   pro-
Lord will pro- vide."
Lord will pro- vide."

vide;   Yes, we'll trust   in   the Lord,   And   he   will   pro - vide.

BEAUTIFUL VALLEY OF EDEN.

No. 78.   "There remaineth, therefore, a rest to the people of God."—Heb. iv: 9.

W. O. CUSHING.   W. F. SHERWIN.

1. Beau- ti - ful val - ley of E - den, Sweet is thy noon-tide calm,
2. O - ver the heart of the mourn-er Shin - eth thy gold- en day,
3. There is the home of my Sav - ior; There, with the blood-washed throng,

O - ver the hearts of the wea - ry, Breathing thy waves of balm,
Waft- ing the songs of the an - gels Down from the far - a - way.
O - ver the highlands of glo - ry Roll- eth the great new song.

Refrain.

Beau- ti-ful val- ley of E - den, Home of the pure and blest,
the pure and blest,

How oft - en a - mid the wild bil - lows I dream of thy rest-sweet rest!

By permission.

WALK IN THE LIGHT.

No. 79.

"If we walk in the light, as he is in the light, we have fellowship one with another, and the blood of Jesus Christ, his Son, cleanseth us from all sin."—1 John i: 7.

W. A. C. $\downarrow. = 63 = 35\frac{1}{2}$ WILBUR A. CHRISTY.

1. List to the voice that is speaking in love, Call-ing to those that are straying;
2. Walk in the light; it is Je-sus who pleads, Earnest-ly seek-ing to guide you,
3. Walk in the light; 'tis the Savior's command, These are the words he has giv- en,

Mes-sage of mer- cy that comes from above, Hear what the Savior is say- ing.
Wandering blindly in night's gloom and shades, Heedless of dangers be - side you.
Leading us on to the long-promised land, Leading from earth up to heav-en.

Chorus.
Walk . . . . in the light, . . .

Walk in the light, O walk in the light, Follow the steps of the Sav-ior;

Walk . . . . in the light, . . .

Walk in the light, O walk in the light, Walk in the light for - ev - er.

By permission.

No. 80.

SHALL WE MEET?

"The ransomed of the Lord shall return and come to Zion with songs and everlasting joy upon their heads."
Isaiah xxx: 10.

HORACE L. HASTINGS. $\quad = 84 = 20$ ELIHU S. RICE.

1. Shall we meet be - yond the riv - er, Where the sur - ges cease to roll?
2. Shall we meet in that blest har-bor When our storm-y voy- age is o'er?
3. Shall we meet in yon - der cit - y, Where the towers of crys-tal shine?
4. Shall we meet with Christ our Sav-ior, When he comes to claim his own?

Where, in all the bright for - ev - er, Sor - row ne'er shall press the soul?
Shall we meet and cast the anchor By the fair, ce - les - tial shore?
Where the walls are all of jas- per, Built by workman- ship di - vine?
Shall we know his bless- ed fav - or, And sit down up - on his throne?

Chorus.

Shall we meet, shall we meet, Shall we meet beyond the riv - er?

Shall we meet be - yond the riv - er, Where the sur - ges cease to roll?

No. 81.

"God so loved the world."—John iii: 16.

Mrs. M. STOCKTON.

♩ = 88 = 18

WM. G. FISCHER.

1. God loved the world of sin - ners lost And ru - ined by the
2. E'en now by faith I claim him mine, The ris - en Son of
3. Love brings the glo- rious full - ness in, And to his saints makes
4. Be - liev - ing souls, re - joic - ing go; There shall to you be
5. Of vic - tory now o'er Sa - tan's power Let all the ran - somed

fall; Sal- va- tion full, at high-est cost, He of- fers free to all.
God; Redemption by his death I find, And cleansing through the blood.
known The blessed rest from ev - ery sin, Through faith in Christ a-lone.
given A glorious foretaste here be - low Of end-less life in heaven.
sing, And triumph in the dy-ing hour Through Christ the Lord our King.

Chorus.

O 'twas love,'twas wondrous love! The love of God to me; It

brought my Sav - ior from a - bove, To die on Cal - va - ry.

JESUS ONLY.

No. 82. "They saw no man, save Jesus only."—Matt. xvii: 8.

HATTIE M. CONREY. ♩ = 76 = 24½ Rev. R. LOWRY.

1. What though clouds are hovering o'er me, And I seem to walk a-lone,
2. What though all my earth-ly jour-ney Bringeth naught but wea-ry hours,
3. What though all my heart is yearning For the loved of long a-go,
4. When I soar to realms of glo-ry, And an en-trance I a-wait,

Long-ing, 'mid my cares and crosses, For the joys that now are flown—
And, in grasp-ing for life's ros-es, Thorns I find in-stead of flowers—
Bit-ter les-sons sad-ly learning From the shad-owy page of woe—
If I whis-per, "Jesus on-ly!" Wide will ope the pearl-y gate;

If I've Je-sus, "Je-sus on-ly," Then my sky will have a gem;
If I've Je-sus, "Je-sus on-ly," I pos-sess a clus-ter rare;
If I've Je-sus, "Je-sus on-ly," He'll be with me to the end;
When I join the heaven-ly cho-rus, And the an-gel hosts I see,

He's a Sun of brightest splendor, And the Star of Beth-le-hem.
He's the "Lil-y of the Val-ley," And the "Rose of Sha-ron" fair.
And, un-seen by mor-tal vis-ion, An-gel bands will o'er me bend.
Pre-cious Je-sus, "Je-sus on-ly," Will my theme of rap-ture be.

No. 83.

"And she had a sister called Mary, which also sat at Jesus' feet and heard his word."—Luke x: 39.

♩ = 100 = 14

T. E. PERKINS.

By permission.

1. Sit - ting at the feet of Je - sus, O what words I hear him say!
2. Sit - ting at the feet of Je - sus, Where can mor-tal be more blest?
3. Bless me, O my Savior! bless me, As I sit low at thy feet;

Hap- py place! so near, so pre - cious! May it find me there each day!
There I lay my sins and sor - rows, And when wea - ry, find sweet rest;
O look down in love up - on me; Let me see thy face so sweet.

Sit - ting at the feet of Je - sus, I would look up- on the past;
Sit - ting at the feet of Je - sus, There I love to weep and pray,
Give me, Lord, the mind of Je - sus, Make me ho - ly, as he is;

For his love has been so gra - cious, It has won my heart at last.
While I from his fullness gath - er Grace and com - fort ev - ery day.
May I prove I've been with Je - sus, Who is all my righteous- ness!

88

YES, BY AND BY.

"And they shall see his face."—Rev. xxii: 4.

No. 84.

♩ = 80 = 22

R. M. McINTOSH.

1. It may be far, it may be near, There is a hope, there is a fear,
2. Impatient soul, and murmuring heart, Your murmuring cease and bear your part
3. Yes, "by and by" will soon be now, And God will wipe each tear-stained brow;
4. O verdant fields! O shining shore! The Lamb of God spreads wide the door;

But in the fu-ture waiting, I Shall Je-sus see, yes, "by and by."
Of pain and la-bor on life's road, For soon 'twill lead thee to thy God.
The Lamb shall feed them from the throne, To liv-ing fountains lead his own.
Ah, golden cit-y, sure-ly I Shall see thy glo-ries "by and by."

Chorus.

By and by, yes, by and by, By and by, yes, by and by;

But in the fu-ture waiting, I Shall Je-sus see, yes, "by and by."
There's pain and la-bor on life's road, But soon 'twill lead thee to thy God.
The Lamb shall feed them from the throne, To liv-ing fountains lead his own.
Ah, gold-en cit-y! sure-ly I Shall see thy glo-ries "by and by."

No. 85.   "Behold, the half was never told me."—Kings x: 7.

P. P. B.   ♩ = 96 — 15¼   P. P. BLISS.

By permission.

1. Re-peat the sto-ry o'er and o'er, Of grace so full and free;
2. Of peace I on-ly knew the name, Nor found my soul its rest,
3. My high-est place is ly-ing low At my Re-deem-er's feet;
4. And O what rap-ture will it be, With all the host a-bove,

I love to hear it more and more, Since grace has res-cued me.
Un-til the sweet-voiced an-gel came To soothe my wea-ry breast.
No re-al joy in life I know, But in his serv-ice sweet.
To sing, through all e-ter-ni-ty, The won-ders of his love.

Chorus.

The half was never told, The half was never told,

The half was nev-er, nev-er told, The half was nev-er, nev-er told,

The half was never told.

1. Of grace divine, so wonder-ful,
2. Of peace, etc.   The half was nev-er, never told.
3. Of joy, etc.
4. Of love, etc.

90

No. 86.

IF I WERE A VOICE.

"As we have therefore opportunity, let us do good to all men."—Gal. vi. 10.

KNOWLES SHAW.

By permission.

1. If I were a voice, a per-suasive voice, That could trav-el this
2. If I were a voice, a con-sol-ing voice, I would fly on the
3. If I were a voice, an im-mor-tal voice That could trav-el this

wide world through, I would fly on the beams of the morning light,
wings of the air; The homes of sor-row and guilt I'd seek,
wide world round; Wher-ev-er man to his i-dols bowed,

I would speak to men with a gen-tle might, I'd tell them to be true.
And calm and truth-ful words I'd speak, To save them from de-spair.
I'd pub-lish, in notes both long and loud, The gos-pel's joy-ful sound.

I would fly, I would fly, o-ver land and sea, Wher-ev-er a
I would fly, I would fly, o'er the crowd-ed town, I'd drop, like the
I would fly, I would fly, on the wings of day, Proclaim-ing peace

human heart could be; Tell-ing a tale, or singing a song, In
happy sun-beam, down In-to the hearts of suffer-ing men, I'd
on my world-wide way; Bid-ding this sad-dened earth re-joice, If

Chorus.

praise of the right, or in blame of the wrong.
teach them to look up a-gain. I would fly, I would
I were a voice, an im-mor-tal voice.

fly, I would fly, I would fly, I would fly o-ver land and sea.

THERE IS A GREEN HILL FAR AWAY.

No. 87.

"And when they were come to the place which is called Calvary, there they crucified him."—Luke xxiii: 33.

Mrs. ALEXANDER.   ♩. = 72 = 27   T. E. PERKINS.

1. There is a green hill far a - way, With-out a cit - y wall,
2. We may not know, we cannot tell What pains he had to bear,
3. He died that we might be for -given, He died to make us good,
4. There was no oth - er good e - nough To pay the price of sin,

Where the dear Lord was cru - ci - fied Who died to save us all.
But we be- lieve it was for us He hung and suf-fered there.
That we might go at last to heaven, Saved by his pre-cious blood.
He on - ly could un - lock the gate Of heaven, and let us in.

Chorus,

O dear -ly, dear - ly has he loved, And we must love him too,

And trust in his re - deem-ing blood, And try his works to do.

Words arranged.   ♩. = 66 = 32   O. R. BARROWS.

1. Gath - ering homeward from ev - ery land, Gath-er - ing one by   one;
2. Loved ones have gone to that dis- tant shore, Gath-er - ing one by   one;
3. We, too, shall come to the riv - er-side, Gath-er - ing one by   one;
4. Je - sus, Re-deem-er, be thou our stay! Gath-er - ing one by   one;

Pilgrims are join-ing the heavenly band, Gath-er - ing one by   one; Their
Oth-ers are go- ing for - ev - er-more,   Gath-er - ing one by   one; Our
Near-er its wa- ters each e - ven-tide,   Gath-er - ing one by   one; O
Cross the dark riv- er with us, we pray, Gath-er - ing one by   one; Then

brows are enclosed in golden crowns,Their travel-stained robes are all laid down,
sisters so gentle,our brothers so brave, The beau-ti - ful children o'er the wave,
Je-sus, our fainting strength uphold, The waves of that river are dark and cold;
bold-ly we'll come to Jordan's side, And fearless - ly breast its swell- ing tide,

Gath-er-ing homeward from ev - ery land, Gath-er- ing one by   one.
Gath-er-ing homeward from ev - ery land, Gath-er- ing one by   one.
Gath-er-ing homeward from ev - ery land, Gath-er- ing one by   one.
Gath-er-ing homeward from ev - ery land, Gath-er- ing one by   one.

Refrain.

Home,   home,   sweet,   sweet home,

Gath-er-ing, gath-er-ing, gath-er-ing home, Gath-er-ing homeward one by one;

Home,   home,   Home, . . .

Gath-er-ing, gath-er-ing, gath-er-ing home, Sweet, sweet home; Gath-er- ing,

home,   sweet,   sweet home,

gath - er - ing, gath - er - ing home, Gath - er - ing homeward one by one;

Home,   home,

Gath - er - ing, gath - er - ing, gath - er - ing home, Sweet, sweet home.

NEARER HOME.

No. 89. "Nearer than when we believed."—Rom. xiii: 11.

UNKNOWN. ♩ = 80 = 22 JAS. McGRANAHAN.

1. O'er the hill the sun is set-ting, And the eve is drawing on;
2. One day near-er, sings the sail-or, As he glides the wa-ters o'er,
3. Worn and wea-ry, oft the pil-grim Hails the set-ting of the sun;
4. Near-er home! yes, one day near-er To our Fa-ther's house on high,

Slow-ly droops the gen-tle twi-light, For an-oth-er day is gone.
While the light is soft-ly dy-ing On his dis-tant na-tive shore.
For the goal is one day near-er, And his jour-ney near-ly done.
To the green fields and the fountains Of the land be-yond the sky.

Gone for aye, its race is o-ver, Soon the dark-er shades will come;
Thus the Christian, on life's o-cean, As his light boat cuts the foam,
Thus we feel, when o'er life's des-ert, Heart and san-dal worn, we roam;
For the heavens grow brighter o'er us, And the lamps hang in the dome,

Still it's sweet to know at e-ven, We are one day near-er home.
In the eve-ning cries with rap-ture, "I am one day near-er home."
As the twi-light gath-ers o'er us, We are one day near-er home.
And our tents are pitched still clos-er, For we're one day near-er home.

Chorus.

Near-er home, near-er home,
beau - ti - ful home, heav - en - ly home,

Near - er to our home on high.
our home on high, near - er to our home on high.

To the green fields and the foun - tains
To the green fields and the fountains, to the green fields and the fountains,

Of the land be-yond the sky.
Of the land be-yond the sky, be-yond the sky, be-yond the sky.

GATHERING HOME.

No. 90. "Gathering together unto him."—2 Thess. ii: 1.

Miss MARIANA B. SLADE. $\textit{d}.=66=32$ R. M. McINTOSH.

1. Up to the boun-ti-ful Giv-er of life, Gathering home! gathering home!
2. Up to the cit - y where falleth no night, Gathering home! gathering home!
3. Up to the beau-ti-ful mansions a- bove, Gathering home! gathering home!

Up to the dwelling where cometh no strife, The dear ones are gath-er-ing home!
Up where the Savior's own face is the light, The dear ones are gath-er-ing home!
Safe in the arms of his in - fi - nite love, The dear ones are gath-er-ing home!

By permission.

Chorus.

Gath-er- ing home, ... Gath-er- ing home, ...
Gath-er- ing home,   Gath-er- ing home,

Nev- er to sorrow more, nev-er to roam, Gath-er-ing home,
Gath-er- ing home,

Gath-er - ing home,   God's children are gath-er - ing home.

Gath-er - ing home,

No. 91.   SOW THE SEED.

"In the morning sow thy seed, and in the evening withhold not thy hand."—Ec. xi: 6.

UNKNOWN.   ♩=80=22   T. C. O'KANE.

1. In   the fur - rows of   thy   life, Sow the seed (good-ly seed);
2. Though thy work should seem to fail, Sow the seed (good-ly seed);
3. Spring-time al - ways dawns for thee, Sow the seed (good-ly seed);

By permission.

Small may be thy spir - it - field, But a good-ly crop 'twill yield;
Some may fall on sto - ny ground, Flower and blade are oft - en found
O - pen then thy gold- en store, Stretch thy fur-rows more and more,

Sow the kind -ly word and deed, Sow the seed, sow the seed, good-ly seed.
In the clefts we lit - tle heed, Sow the seed, sow the seed, good-ly seed.
God will give thee all thy need, Sow the seed, sow the seed, good-ly seed.

No. 92. WATCH.

"And at midnight there was a cry made, Behold, the bridegroom cometh; go ye out to meet him."—Matt. xxv: 6.

Miss. MARIANA B. SLADE. ♩=96 = 15¼ R. M. McINTOSH.

1. When the cry shall be made at the mid-night, "Go ye out, for the
2. Till he comes, now he bids us be read - y; Can you say to the
3. O how sad if our oil is all wast -ed, Though we hast - en our
4. O when ris - es the glo - ri - ous summons, "Meet the Bridegroom and

Bride-groom is near!" Will you rise, with your lamps trimmed and burning?
Bride-groom, I am? Will you en - ter the door that is o - pen,
lamps to re- new; If we find that the Bride-groom has en-tered,
join in the song!" May we all, with our lamps bright-ly burn -ing,

Refrain.

Will you joy - ful - ly bid him draw near?
To the dear mar-riage feast of the Lamb? We will watch, we will
Left without, then O what shall we do?
En- ter in with the wor- ship-ping throng. We will watch, ev - er

watch, Till the Bridegroom shall come in his power; Jesus saith,
watch, we will watch, Jesus saith,

we must watch,   For we know not the day nor the hour.
ev - er watch,

No. 93.   **PASS ME NOT.**

"Whosoever shall call upon the name of the Lord shall be saved."—Rom. x: 13.

F. C. VAN ALSTYNE.   ♩ = 88 = 18   W. H. DOANE.

1. Pass me not, O gen- tle Sav - ior! Hear my hum-ble cry; While on
2. Let me at thy throne of mer- cy Find a sweet re - lief; Kneel-ing
3. Trusting on - ly in thy mer - it, Would I seek thy face; Heal my
4. Thou the Spring of all my com-fort, More than life to me, Whom on

Chorus.

oth - ers thou art smil - ing, Do not pass me by.
there in deep con - tri - tion, Help my un - be - lief. Sav-ior, Sav -ior,
wounded, bro - ken spir - it, Save me by thy grace.
earth have I be- side thee, Whom in heaven but thee?

hear my humble cry! While on oth-ers thou art call- ing, Do not pass me by.

CLEFT FOR ME.

No. 94.

"As the shadow of a great rock in a weary land."—Isa. xxxii: 2.

FANNY CROSBY.   ♩=84=20   T. C. O'KANE.

1. Might - y Rock, whose towering form Looks a - bove the frowning storm;
2. Of the springs that from thee burst, Let me drink and quench my thirst;
3. When I near the stream of death, When I feel its chill- y breath,

Rock, a - mid the des - ert waste, To thy shad - ow now I haste.
Wea - ry, faint- ing, toil - oppressed, In thy shad - ow let me rest.
Rock, where all my hopes a - bide, In thy shad - ow let me hide.

Refrain.

Un - to thee, un - to thee, Pre-cious Sav - ior, now I flee;

"Rock of a - ges, cleft for me, Let me hide my- self in thee."

No. 95.

"In the shadow of thy wings will I make my refuge until these calamities are overpast."—Ps. lvii: 1.

CHARLES WESLEY.   ♩ = 69 = 29½   J. P. HOLBROOK.

1. Je - sus, lov - er of my soul, Let me to thy bo - som fly,
2. Oth - er ref - uge have I none, Hangs my help - less soul on thee;
3. Thou, O Christ, art all I want; Boundless love in thee I find;
4. Plenteous grace with thee is found, Grace to par - don all my sin:

While the bil - lows near me roll, While the tem - pest still is high;
Leave, O leave me not a - lone! Still sup - port and com-fort me.
Raise the fall - en, cheer the faint, Heal the sick, and lead the blind.
Let the heal - ing streams abound, Make and keep me pure with- in.

Hide me, O my Sav-ior, hide, Till the storm of life is past;
All my trust on thee is stayed, All my help from thee I bring;
Just and ho - ly is thy name, Prince of peace and right-eous-ness;
Thou of life the fountain art, Free - ly let me take of thee;

Safe in - to the ha - ven guide; O re - ceive my soul at last!
Cov - er my de-fense-less head With the shad - ow of thy wing.
Most un-wor-thy, Lord, I am; Thou art full of love and grace.
Spring thou up with-in my heart, Rise to all e - ter - ni - ty.

IN THE CROSS OF CHRIST WE GLORY.

No. 96.

"God forbid that I should glory, save in the cross of our Lord Jesus Christ."—Gal. vi: 14.

SIR JOHN BOWRING. ♩ = 104 = 13 G. M. COLE.

1. In the cross of Christ we glo-ry, Tower-ing o'er the wrecks of time;
2. When the woes of life o'er-take us, Hopes deceive, and fears an- noy,
3. Bane and bless- ing, pain and pleasure, By the cross are sanc - ti - fied;

All the light of sa - cred sto- ry Gath - ers 'round its head sub-lime.
Nev - er shall the cross for-sake us; Lo! it glows with peace and joy.
Peace is there that knows no mea-sure, Joys that through all time a - bide.

By permission.

Chorus.

'Tis the cross of our sal - va- tion, May we love it more and more,

And, with heavenly ex - ul - ta - tion, Sing its glo - ries o'er and o'er.

No. 97.

"It is I; be not afraid."—Matt. xiv: 27.

Rev. J. PARKER. $\quad \bullet_{\bullet} = 52 = 52 \quad$ W. G. FISCHER.

By permission.

1. Fear not the gloom of the mid- night, Dread not the storm of the sea;
2. Fear not the gloom of the fur - nace, The Mas-ter is speaking to thee;
3. Heed not the wrath of the tempt - er, My pres-ence thy shel-ter shall be;
4. Fear not the chill of the val - ley, For death but a shad-ow shall be;

'Tis I who am com-ing to save thee, 'Tis I! art thou trusting in me?
'Tis I who am cool-ing the foot-steps, 'Tis I! art thou trusting in me?
'Tis I who am keeping thy spir - it, 'Tis I! art thou trusting in me?
My rod and my staff shall support thee, 'Tis I! keep on trusting in me.

Chorus.

Trusting in thee, yes, trusting in thee, I'll doubt thee no more, my Re-deem-er;

Yes, trusting in thee, yes, trusting in thee, I'll ev - er be trusting in thee.

No. 98. WAITING AND WATCHING.

"Watch, therefore; for ye know not what hour your Lord doth come."—Matt. xxiv: 42.

S. M. H.   ♩. = 63 = 35½   WILL H. PONTIUS.

By permission.

1. We know not the time when he com - eth, At e - ven, or
2. I think of his won - der - ful pit - y, The price our sal -
   O Je - sus, my lov - ing Re - deem-er, Thou know-est I

mid- night, or morn; It may be at deep - en - ing twi-light,
va - tion hath cost; He left the bright man-sions of glo - ry
cher - ish as dear The hope that mine eyes shall be - hold thee,

It may be at ear - li - est dawn. He bids us to
To suf - fer and die for the lost. And some-times I
That I shall thine own wel - come hear. If to some as a

watch and be read - y, Nor suf - fer our lights to grow dim;
think it will please him, When those whom he died to re - deem,
judge thou ap - pear-est, Who forth from thy presence would flee,

That, when he may come, he will find us All wait - ing and
Re - joice in the hope of his com -ing, By wait - ing and
A Friend most be - lov - ed I'll greet thee; I'm wait - ing and

Chorus.

watch-ing for him. Wait - ing and watch - ing,
watch-ing for him. Wait - ing and watching, yes, waiting for him(thee*),
watch-ing for him(thee*),

Wait - - ing and watch - ing, Wait -
Wait - ing and watching, yes, wait - ing for him(thee*), Wait- ing and

Repeat pp.

ing and watch - ing, Still wait-ing and watching for him(thee*).
watch-ing, yes, wait-ing and watching,

* For last verse.

SHOUT THE TIDINGS.

No. 99.

"Go ye into all the world and preach the gospel to every creature."—Mark xvi: 15.

UNKNOWN.　　　　　　　　♩ = 104 = 13　　　　　　　W. B. BRADBURY.

1. Shout the tid-ings of sal - va - tion　To the a - ged and the young,
2. Shout the tid-ings of sal - va - tion　O'er the prairies of the west,
3. Shout the tid-ings of sal - va - tion,　Ming- ling with the o- cean's roar,
4. Shout the tid-ings of sal - va - tion　O'er the islands of the sea,

Till the precious in - vi - ta - tion　Wak- en ev- ery heart and tongue.
Till each gathering congre - ga - tion　With the gos-pel sound is blest.
Till the ships of ev - ery na - tion　Bear the news from shore to shore.
Till, in hum-ble a - do - ra - tion,　All to Christ shall bow the knee.

Chorus.

Send the sound the earth around, From the rising to the set-ting of the sun,

Till each gathering crowd shall proclaim a - loud, The glo- rious work is done.

No. 100. "And his windows being open in his chamber toward Jerusalem."—Dan. vi: 10.

P. P. B.   ♩=88=18   P. P. BLISS.

1. Do you see the Hebrew captive kneeling, At morning, noon and night to pray?
2. Do not fear to tread the fiery fur-nace, Nor shrink the lion's den to share;
3. Children of the living God, take courage; Your great deliverance sweetly sing;

In his chamber he remembers Zi - on, Though in ex - ile far a-way.
For the God of Dan-iel will de - liv - er, He will send his an- gel there.
Set your fa - ces to the hill of Zi - on, Thence to hail our com-ing King!

Chorus.

Are your windows open toward Jerusalem, Though as captives here a "little while" we

stay? For the coming of the King in his glory, Are you watching day by day?

TRUST IN THE LORD.

No. 101.

"It is better to trust in the Lord than to put confidence in princes."—Ps. cxviii: 9.

W. F. S.　　　♩ = 104 = 13　　　W. F. SHERWIN.

1. It is bet-ter to trust in the Lord, Than to lean on the waver - ing arm
2. It is bet-ter to trust in the Lord, For the word of his promise is sure;
3. It is bet-ter to trust in the Lord, Rest-ing firm in his in - fi - nite love;

Ot the kings and the princes of earth; God a - lone is a re-fuge from harm.
Tho' the way may be rugged and dark, There are bright crowns for those who en-dure.
And with gladness to serve him below, Till we en - ter his kingdom a - bove.

By permission.

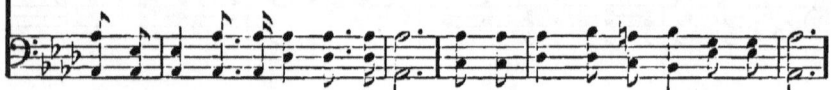

Refrain.

Trust the Lord,　　　O trust in the Lord; Low at his feet let us fall!
trust the Lord,

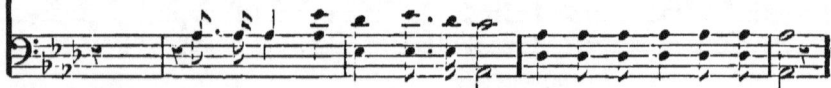

Trust the Lord,　　　O trust in the Lord, For he is the King o-ver all.
trust the Lord,

WILL JESUS FIND US WATCHING?

"Watch therefore; for ye know not what hour your Lord doth come."—Matt. xxiv: 42.

FANNY J. CROSBY. ♩ = 100 = 14 W. H. DOANE.

1. When Jesus comes to reward his serv-ants, Whether it be noon or night,
2. If at the dawn of the ear-ly morn-ing He shall call us one by one,
3. Have we been true to the trust he left us? Do we seek to do our best?
4. Blessed are those whom the Lord finds watching, In his glo-ry they shall share;

Rit,

Faith-ful to him will he find us watching, With our lamps all trimmed and bright?
When to the Lord we restore our tal-ents, Will he an-swer thee—Well done?
If in our hearts there is naught condemns us, We shall have a glo-rious rest.
If he shall come at the dawn or midnight, Will he find us watching there?

Refrain,

O can we say we are read-y, broth-er? Ready for the soul's bright home?

Say will he find you and me still watching, Waiting, waiting when the Lord shall come?

WHO WILL MEET ME THERE?

No. 103.

"For the Lamb * * shall lead them unto living fountains of waters."—Rev. vii: 17.

FANNY J. CROSBY.   ♩ = 92 = 16½   W. H. DOANE.

1. When my journey past, I am safe at last At the gate of life so fair,
2. Friends that left me here, Hearts that held me dear, Call me to their home of song;
3. To the golden shore Thou wilt bear me o'er, I shall feel thy ten-der care;

Who will take my hand In the spir-it land? Who will come to meet me there?
But, to find my rest, Ev-er on thy breast, Draws me with a love so strong.
Thou wilt take my hand In the spir-it land, Thou wilt bid me welcome there.

Refrain.

When the morn-ing bright Fills my soul with light, Jesus, let me look on thee;

Lov-ing Savior mine, Let thy voice di-vine Be the first to welcome me.

GALILEE.

"Jesus departed thence and came nigh unto the sea of Galilee."—Matt. xv: 29.

R. MORRIS, D.D., LL. D.

R. M. McINTOSH.

1. Each coo - ing dove and sigh - ing bough, That makes the eve so blest to me,
2. Each flow-ery glen and moss - y dell, Where hap - py birds in song a - gree,
3. And when I read the thrill-ing love Of him who walked up-on the sea,

Has something far di - vin - er now; It bears me back to Gal -i - lee.
Through sun- ny morn the prais- es tell Of sights and sounds in Gal -i - lee.
I long, O how I long once more To fol - low him in Gal -i - lee.

Chorus.

O Gal - i - lee, sweet Gal - i - lee, Where Je- sus loved so much to be;

O Gal - i - lee, blue Gal - i- lee, Come, sing thy song a - gain to me.

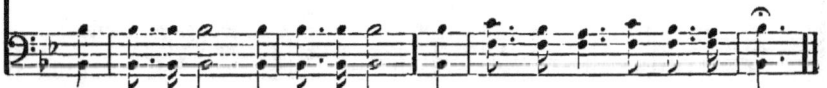

By permission.

112 No. 105.

HIDING IN THEE.

"My strong rock, for a house of defense, to save me."—Ps. xxxi. 2

Rev. W. O. CUSHING.

♩ = 112 = 11¼

IRA D. SANKEY.

1. O safe to the Rock that is high - er than I, My soul,
2. In the calm of the noon- tide, in sor-row's lone hour, In times
3. How oft in the con - flict, when pressed by the foe, I have fled

like a bird that is wounded, would fly; So sin - ful, so wea-ry, O
when temp-ta - tion casts o'er me its power; In the tem-pests of life, on its
to my ref-uge and breathed out my woe; How oft when my tri - als like

thine would I be; Thou blest "Rock of A-ges," I'm hid - ing in thee.
wide, heaving sea, O blest "Rock of A-ges," I'm hid - ing in thee.
bil-lows would roll, I have hid- den in thee, O thou Rock of my soul!

Refrain.

Hid - ing in thee, hid - ing in thee, Thou blest "Rock of Ages," I'm hiding in thee.

Copyright, 1877, by Biglow & Main. Used by permission.

DRAW ME NEARER.

"Let us draw near with a true heart."—Heb. x: 22.

FANNY J. CROSBY. ♩=88=18 W. H. DOANE.

1. I am thine, O Lord, I have heard thy voice, And it told thy love to me;
2. Conse-crate me now to thy serv-ice, Lord, By the power of grace di-vine;
3. O the pure de-light of a sin - gle hour That be-fore thy throne I spend,
4. There are depths of love that I can not know Till I cross the nar-row sea;

But I long to rise in the arms of faith, And be clos- er drawn to thee.
Let my soul look up with a steadfast hope, And my will be lost in thine.
When I kneel in prayer, and with thee, my God, I commune as friend with friend!
There are heights of joy that I may not reach Till I rest in peace with thee.

Refrain.

Draw me near - er, near-er, blessed Lord, To the cross where thou hast died;
near-er, near-er,

Draw me near-er, near-er, nearer, blessed Lord, To thy precious, bleeding side.

114 No. 107.

ARE YOU READY?

"Therefore, be ye also ready."—Matt. xxiv: 44.

J. W. SLAUGHENHAUPT.   ♩ = 84 = 20   E. S. LORENZ.

1. Soon the evening shadows falling Close the day of mor-tal life: Soon the
2. Soon the awful trumpet sounding Calls thee to the judgment throne; Now pre-
3. O how fa-tal 'tis to lin-ger! Are you read-y—read-y now? Read-y,
4. Priceless love and free sal-va-tion Free-ly still are of-fered thee; Yield no

Refrain.

hand of death appalling Draws thee from its weary strife.
pare, for love abounding Yet has left thee not alone. Are you ready?
should death's i-cy finger Lay its chill up-on thy brow?   Are you ready?
long-er to temp-ta-tion, But from sin and sorrow flee.

by permission.

Are you read-y (are you ready)? 'Tis the Spir-it calling, why de-lay? Are you

ready (are you ready)? Are you ready (are you ready)? Do not linger longer, come to-day.

I HAVE A SWEET HOPE.

"I will come again and receive you unto myself."—John xiv: 3.

Rev. J. H. MARTIN.   ♩. = 66 = 32   Dr. A. B. EVERETT.

1. I have a sweet hope that in heav-en a-bove The Sav-ior is wait-ing for
2. In midst of the troubles and sor-rows I bear, By faith I re-pose on his
3. He's gone to prepare for his peo-ple a place—A man-sion of glo-ry on
4. I know when this bod-y of flesh shall de-cay My strength and my portion he'll

me,—That, ran-somed and saved by his mer-cy and love, My friend and my
breast; I know he will make my af-flic-tions his care, And bring me at
high; And when I shall fin-ish my jour-ney and race, He'll give me a
be; In death he will be my sweet comfort and stay: The Sav-ior is

Chorus.

por-tion he'll be.
last to his rest.   Je-sus, dear Je-sus will wel-come me, Wel-come me,
home in the sky.
wait-ing for me.

wel-come me; Jesus, dear Jesus will welcome me Home to the beautiful land.

116

No. 109.

THE KINGDOM COMING.

"Thy kingdom come."—Matt. vi: 10.

Mrs. M. B. C. SLADE.　　♩= 84 = 20　　R. M McINTOSH.

1. From all the dark pla - ces Of earth's heathen ra - ces, O see how the
2. The sun-light is glancing O'er ar- mies ad-vanc-ing, To con-quer the
3. With shouting and singing, And ju - bi - lant ring-ing, Their arms of re-

thick shadows fly! The voice of sal - va - tion Awakes ev - ery na - tion,
king-doms of sin; Our Lord shall possess them, His presence shall bless them,
bel - lion cast down, At last ev-ery na - tion The Lord of sal - va - tion,

Chorus.

Come o - ver and help us, they cry.
His beau-ty shall en-ter them in. The kingdom is com-ing, O tell ye the
Their King and Redeemer, shall crown!

sto - ry, God's ban-ner ex - alt- ed shall be! The earth shall be full of

His knowledge and glo - ry, As wa - ters that cov - er the sea!

No. 110. **ROCK-SHADOW.**

"The shadow of a great rock in a weary land."—Isa. xxxii: 2.

RAY PALMER. $\quad \bullet = 69 = 29\frac{1}{2}$ T. C. O'KANE.

1. { In the shad- ow of the Rock Let me rest, let me rest,
   { When I feel the tem- pest shock Thrill my breast, thrill my breast;
2. { On the parched and des-ert way, Where I tread, where I tread,
   { With the noontide, scorching ray O'er my head, o'er my head,
3. { I in peace will rest me there Till I see, till I see,
   { That the skies a - gain are fair O - ver me, o - ver me;
4. { Then my pil- grim staff I'll take, And once more, and once more
   { I'll my on-ward jour - ney make, As be - fore, as be - fore;

All in vain the storm shall sweep While I hide, while I hide,
Let me find the wel-come shade, Cool and still, cool and still,
That the burn- ing heats are past, And the day, and the day,
And with joy- ous heart and strong, I will raise, I will raise

And my tran-quil sta - tion keep By thy side, by thy side.
And my wea - ry steps be stayed Where I will, where I will.
Bids the wea - ry 'one at last Go his way, go his way.
Un - to thee, O Rock, a song Glad with praise, glad with praise.

By permission.

No. 111.

A victim of consumption, having gone to a distant State in quest of health, was imformed by the physician that he could survive only a few days. He immediately took the train for his distant home, and as he felt the tide of life fast ebbing away, he would frequently inquire of his attendants: "Is it far?" This touching incident suggested the song below to its author.]

KNOWLES SHAW.   ♩=88=18   KNOWLES SHAW.

1. Is it far to the land of rest, Where the wea - ry feet shall
2. Is it far to that peaceful shore, Where the ach- ing heart shall
3. Is it far to the plains of light, To that cit - y with its

nev - er, nev - er roam; To the mansions of the pure and the blest,
sor -row not a - gain; Where the friends who meet shall part nev-er- more,
jas - per walls a - glow, Where the glo - ry of the Lord is the light?

By permission.

Chorus

Where we all shall meet at home? Is it far? is it
But with Christ for - ev - er reign? Is it far to that beau-ti - ful
To that home, say, will you go?

far? Will you tell me, broth-er pil - grim, is it
home of the blest?

far   (is   it   far)?   To   that   man-sion   of   the   blest,   Where   the

wea - ry   are   at   rest?   O   say, broth-er   pil - grim,   is   it   far?

No. 112.   **PRAYER.**

"All my springs are in thee."—Ps. lxxxvii: 7,

Miss H. M. WILLIAMS.   ♩ = 80 = 22   T. J. COOK.

1. While thee I   seek, pro - tect-ing Power,Be   my vain   wish-es stilled;
2. In   each e - vent of   life, how clear Thy rul - ing hand I see!
3 In   ev - ery joy   that crowns my days, In   ev - ery pain I bear,
4. My lift - ed eye, with - out a   tear, The gathering storm shall see;

And may this con - se - crat-ed hour With bet - ter hopes be filled.
Each bless- ing to   my   soul more dear, Be - cause con - ferred by thee.
My heart shall find de - light in praise, Or seek re - lief in prayer.
My stead-fast heart shall ban-ish fear; That heart shall rest on thee.

ONLY WAITING.

No. 113.

"Having a desire to depart, and to be with Christ, which is far better."—Phil. i: 23.

W. G. IRVIN.   ♩=92=16½   J. H. FILLMORE.

1. I am waiting for the morn-ing   Of the bless-ed day to dawn,
2. I am waiting, worn and wea-ry,   With the bat-tle and the strife,
3. Waiting, hoping, trusting ev - er,   For a home of boundless love,
4. Waiting for the sun to cheer me   With his pure, un-min-gled light,

When the sor-row and the sad - ness   Of this fear-ful life are gone.
Hop-ing, when the war is end - ed,   To re-ceive a crown of life.
Like a pilgrim looking for - ward   To the land of bliss a - bove,
Wait-ing for the saints to greet me   In their robes of spotless white.

Chorus.

I am wait - - - - - - - ing, on - ly wait-ing,
I am wait-ing, wait-ing, wait-ing, on - ly waiting, waiting, waiting,

Till this wea - - - - - - - ry life is o'er,
Till this wea-ry, wea-ry, wea - ry life is o'er, life is o'er,

On - ly wait - - - - - - - - - - ing for my wel - come,
On - ly wait - ing, wait - ing, wait - ing for my wel - come, for

my wel - come, From my Sav - ior on the oth - er shore.

No. 114. **ALETTA.**

"Take my yoke upon you, and learn of me."—Matt. xi: 29.

UNKNOWN. $\quad \bullet = 84 = 20$ WM. B. BRADBURY.

By permission.

1. Sav-ior! teach me, day by day, Love's sweet les - son to o - bey;
2. With a child-like heart of love, At thy bid- ding may I move;
3. Teach me all thy steps to trace, Strong to fol - low in thy grace;
4. Love in lov - ing finds em- ploy— In o - be-dience all her joy;

Sweet - er les - son can not be, Lov- ing him who first loved me.
Prompt to serve and fol - low thee, Lov- ing him who first loved me.
Learn - ing how to love from thee, Lov- ing him who first loved me.
Ev - er new that joy will be, Lov- ing him who first loved me.

No. 115.

COMING BY AND BY.

"It shall come to pass in the last days."—Isa. ii: 2.

R. L.

♩ = 92 = 16½

R. LOWRY.

1. A bet - ter day is coming, A morning promised long, When girded
2. The boast of haughty er - ror No more will fill the air, But age and
3. O for that ho - ly dawning We watch, and wait, and pray, Till o'er the

right, with ho - ly might, Will o - ver-throw the wrong; When God the Lord will
youth will love the truth, And spread it ev - ery-where; No more from want and
height the morn-ing light Shall drive the gloom a-way; And when the heaven-ly

list - en To ev - ery plain-tive sigh, And stretch his hand o'er ev - ery land
sor-row Will come the hope-less cry; And strife will cease, and per-fect peace
glo -ry Shall flood the earth and sky, We'll bless the Lord for all his word,

Refrain.

With jus - tice by and by.
Will flour-ish by and by. Com-ing by and by, coming by and by,
And praise him by and by.

The bet-ter day is coming, The morning draweth nigh;Coming by and by,

coming by and by! The welcome dawn will hasten on, 'Tis coming by and by.

No. 116. SOON AND FOREVER.

"The time is short."—1 Cor. vii: 29.

P. P. BLISS. ♩. = 60 = 39 P. P. BLISS.

1. On - ly a few more years, On - ly a few more cares,
2. On - ly a few more wrongs, On - ly a few more sighs,
3. Then an e - ter - nal stay, Then an e - ter - nal throng,

On - ly a few more smiles and tears, On - ly a few more prayers;
On - ly a few more earth-ly songs, On - ly a few good - byes;
Then an e - ter - nal, glo - rious day, Then an e - ter - nal song.

No. 117.

THROUGH THE JORDAN.

"When thou passest through the waters I will be with thee; and through the rivers, they shall not overflow thee."— Isa. xliii: 2.

W. F. S.   ♩ = 96 = 15¼   W. F. SHERWIN.

1. Sing a- loud a joy- ful cho-rus! Come with re-joic-ing, Prais-ing him who
2. When thou passest through the waters, I will be with thee, They shall not o'er-
3. Through the flames, if Jesus calls us, We'll go with singing, Where-so-e'er he

guid-ed his peo-ple of old; For the God who led the fathers Liv-eth for-
flow thee nor give thee a-larm; Lo! the Ho - ly One of Is- rael, Mighty to
lead-eth we fear not to stand. Trusting in the blessed promise, "I'm with you

Chorus.

ev - er, And in ten- der mer- cy doth the children behold.
save thee, Guardeth still the loved ones who will lean on his arm. Through the Jordan,
always, Till you reach the mansions of the fair promised land."

through the Jor - - dan, We will go when he gives us the word (the word);
through the Jor-dan,

By permission.

In the Jor-dan, in the Jor - - dan, We are safe with the ark of the Lord.
In the Jor-dan,

No. 118.   PRAISE TO OUR CREATOR.

"With my song will I praise him."—Ps. xxviii: 7.

By permission.

FAWCETT.   ♩. = 60 = 39   T. C. O'KANE.

1. Praise to thee, our great Creator, Praise be thine from ev-ery tongue; Join, my soul, with
2. Fa-ther, source of all compassion, Free, unbounded love is thine; Hail the God of
3.   Joy-ful- ly on earth adore him, Till in heaven our song we raise; There enraptured

Chorus.

ev-ery creature, Join the   u- ni- ver- sal song.
our sal - va-tion, Praise him for his love di- vine. Praise him for his mer - cy,
fall be- fore him, Lost in   wonder, love and praise.

Praise him ev-ery   day; For his boundless goodness, Ev-er praise and pray.

126

No. 119.

HO! REAPERS OF LIFE'S HARVEST.

"The harvest truly is plenteous, but the laborers are few."—Matt. ix: 37.

I. B. W.

$\quad = 96 — 15\frac{1}{4}$

I. B. WOODBURY.

1. Ho! reap - ers of life's har - vest, Why stand with rust - ed blade,
2. Thrust in your sharp-ened sic - kle, And gath - er in the grain,
3. Come down from hill and moun-tain In morn-ing's rud- dy glow,
4. Mount up the heights of wis - dom, And crush each er - ror low;

Un - til the night draws round thee, And day be - gins to fade?
The night is fast ap - proaching, And soon will come a - gain.
Nor wait un - til the di - al Points to the noon be - low;
Keep back no words of knowledge That hu - man hearts should know.

Why stand ye i - dle, wait- ing For reap - ers more to come?
The Mas - ter calls for reap- ers, And shall he call in vain?
And come with strong -er sin - ew, Nor faint in heat or cold,
Be faith - ful to thy mis - sion, In serv - ice of thy Lord,

The gold - en morn is pass - ing, Why sit ye i - dle, dumb?
Shall sheaves lie there un - gath - ered, And waste up - on the plain?
And pause not till the evening Draws round its wealth of gold.
And then a gold - en chap - let Shall be thy just re - ward.

By permission.

No. 120.

THE PLACE PREPARED.

"I go to prepare a place for you."—John xiv: 2.

Mrs. M. B. C. SLADE. $\bullet. = 60 = 29\frac{1}{2}$ R. M. McINTOSH.

1. There's a beauti - ful place for you and for me, We homeless shall be never-more;
2. And I need not look off to find the dear place, O'er Jordan's dark rolling away;
3. I shall en-ter his house and find him, I know, In do- ing the will of his word;

For a mansion prepared by Je -sus I see, And he is the Way and the Door.
For he calleth me nigh, and shows me his face, And bids me be welcome to - day.
In my heav-en-ly home be-gun here be-low, I'll dwell ev- er-more with my Lord.

Beau-ti-ful home! beauti-ful home! Sing-ing its sto-ry I tell,
beautiful home! beautiful home!

O en-ter, my soul, no long-er to roam, For- ev - er with Je- sus to dwell.

WHILE THE DAYS ARE GOING BY.

No. 121.

"Whatsoever thy hand findeth to do, do with thy might."—Eccles. ix: 10.

GEORGE COOPER.   ♩ = 84 = 20   IRA D. SANKEY.

1. There are lone - ly hearts to cher - ish, While the days are go- ing by;
2. There's no time for i - dle scorn- ing, While the days are go- ing by;
3. All the lov - ing links that bind us, While the days are go- ing by,

There are wea - ry souls who per - ish, While the days are go- ing by;
Let your face be like the morn-ing, While the days are go- ing by;
One by one we leave be-hind us, While the days are go- ing by;

If a smile we can re - new, As our jour - ney we pur - sue,
O the world is full of sighs, Full of sad and weep-ing eyes;
But the seeds of good we sow, Both in shade and shine will grow,

O the good we all may do, While the days are go- ing by.
Help your fall - en broth- er rise, While the days are go- ing by.
And will keep our hearts a - glow, While the days are go- ing by.

Refrain.

Go- ing by (going by), go- ing by(go-ing by),Go- ing by (going by), go-ing

by(go-ing by),   O the good we all may do,While the days are going   by.

No. 122.

ST. SYLVESTER.

"My son, give me thine heart."—Prov. xxiii: 26.

UNKNOWN.   ♩ = 66 = 32   J. B. DYKES.

1. Take my heart, O   Fa-ther! mold it   In   o - be-dience to   thy will;
2. Fa- ther, keep it   pure and low- ly, Strong and brave, yet free from strife,
3. Ev - er   let thy might sur-round it; Strength-en   it   with power di- vine.

And,   as ripen-ing years un - fold it,   Keep it true and child- like still.
Turn - ing from the paths un - ho - ly   Of   a vain or   sin - ful life.
Till   thy cords of love have bound it, Fa- ther,whol - ly un - to thine.

No. 123.

BLESS THE LORD, O MY SOUL.

"—and forget not all his benefits.—Ps. ciii: 2.

Mrs. M. A. KIDDER. $\cdot = 108 = 12,$ R. LOWRY.

1. In the church of the Lord, In the house of our King, We have gathered to
2. We are hap-py to-day, As we sit at the feet Of the bless-ed Re-

worship—To pray and to sing; May our hearts be inspired Our Redeemer to see,
deemer We come here to meet; And a cho-rus of joy As a tribute we bring,

Chorus.

While we all come be-fore him With sweet mel-o-dy. Bless the Lord, ...
With a lov-ing de-vo-tion, To Je-sus, our King.   Bless the Lord,

Bless the Lord, ... Bless the Lord, ... O my soul, O my soul!
Bless the Lord,   Bless the Lord,

And for-get not his ben -e - fits, And for-get not his ben - e - fits;

Bless the Lord, O my soul (O my soul), Bless the Lord, O my soul!

No. 124. **ELIZABETHTOWN.**

"Unto you who believe, he is precious."—1 Pet. ii: 7.

PHILIP DODDRIDGE. ♩ = 66 = 32 GEORGE KINGSLEY.

1. Je - sus, I love thy charm-ing name; 'Tis mu - sic to my ear;
2. Yes, thou art pre- cious to my soul, My transport and my trust;
3. All that my ar - dent soul can wish, In thee doth rich -ly meet;
4. Thy grace shall dwell up - on my heart, And shed its fragrance there—

Fain would I sound it out so loud That all the earth might hear.
Jew - els to thee are gaud - y toys, And gold is sor - did dust.
Nor to my eyes is light so dear, Nor friendship half so sweet.
The no-blest balm of all its wounds, The cor - dial of its care.

No. 125.

HOW ARE YOU LIVING?

"Whether we live, we live unto the Lord."—Rom. xiv: 8.

Rev. E. A. HOFFMAN.   ♩ = 96 = 15¼   R. M. McINTOSH.

1. How: O how are you liv - ing, my broth - er, Are you go - ing the
2. Earth will of - fer you pleasures, my broth - er, Have you turned from these
3. Sin will sure - ly en - tice you, my broth - er, Quick-ly turn from temp-
4. You may grow cold and care - less, my broth - er, And from Christ and his

pilgrim-age way? Are you do- ing the will of your Mas-ter? Are you
pleasures a - way? Are you striving to work for the Mas-ter? Are you
ta-tion a - way; O then give all your life to the Mas-ter, And be
fol-low-ing stray; Are you watching, and praying, and trusting? Are you

Refrain.

liv - ing for Je - sus to - day? Are you liv - ing for Je - sus to-

day, to - day? Are you liv - ing for Je - sus to - day? O tell me, my friend and my broth - er, Are you liv - ing for Je - sus to - day?

No. 126.   **WHITNEY.**

"Unto thee will I cry, O Lord, my Rock."—Ps. xxviii: 1.

UNKNOWN.   ♩. = 50 = 56   LOWELL MASON—Arr.

1. Sweet is the prayer whose ho - ly stream In earn - est
2. Faith grasps the bless - ings she de - sires, Hope points the
3. But sweet - er far the still small voice, Heard by no
4. Nor ac - cents flow, nor words as - cend; All ut - t'rance

plead - ing flows; De - vo - tion dwells up - on the theme,
up - ward gaze; And love, un - trem - bling love, in - spires
hu - man ear, When God hath made the heart re - joice,
fail - eth there; But God him - self doth com - pre - hend,

And warm and warm - er glows, And warm and warm - er glows.
The el - o-quence of praise, The el - o - quence of praise.
And dried the bit - ter tear, And dried the bit - ter tear.
And hear th' un-end - ed prayer, And hear th' un-end - ed prayer.

No. 127. THE FOUNDATION STONE.

"Behold, I lay in Zion a chief corner-stone."—1 Pet ii: 6.

TRACY CLINTON. ♩ = 88 = 18 T. C. O'KANE.

1. Be- hold, a stone in Zi - on laid, A tried, a sure founda-tion stone;
2. Storms may a - rise, and tem-pests blow, And beat with fu-ry on this Rock,
3. Ne'er shall the gates of hell pre-vail O'er those who in the Lord a - bide;

Thrice blest are they whose hopes are staid Up - on this base, and
Still it re-mains, though waves o'er-flow, Un - moved a - mid the
Safe - ly they dwell, though foes as - sail, For - ev - er near the

Chorus.

this a - lone.
fierc-est shock. Some build their hopes on the ev - er drift- ing sand,
Sav-ior's side.

Some on their fame, or their treas-ure, or their land : Mine's on a Rock that for - ev - er will stand, Je - sus, the "Rock of A - ges."

No. 128.   O HOW I LOVE JESUS.

" We love him, because he first loved us."—1 John iv: 19.

Arranged.

By permission.

1. Je-sus, I love thy charming name,'Tis music to my ear; Fain would I
2. Yes,thou art pre-cious to my soul,My transport and my trust; Jewels to
3. All that my ar-dent soul can wish, In thee doth rich - ly meet; Nor to my
4. Thy grace shall dwell upon my heart,And shed its fragrance there;The noblest

Chorus.

sound it out so loud.That all the earth might hear.
thee are gau - dy toys, And gold is sor - did dust.   O how I love Je-sus!
eyes is light so dear,Nor friendship half so sweet.
balm of all its wounds.The cordial of its care.

O how I love Je-sus! O how I love Je-sus! Because he first loved me.

No. 129.

I WILL TRUST IN MY SAVIOR.

"Ye believe in God, believe also in me."—John xiv: 1.

Mrs. LOULA K. ROGERS. ♩ = 88 = 18 R. M. McINTOSH.

1. Though the shadows gather o'er my pathway here, And no sun comes with joyous ray,
2. In the tempest when the winds around me roll, And the thunders my heart affright,
3. When the chilling blight of death is on my brow, And the earth passes from my view,

In the darkness not an e - vil will I fear, For my Sav-ior is leading the way.
Sweetly comes a lov-ing whisper to my soul, Then the world is all beauty and light.
Simply trusting in my Sav-ior then, as now, He will lead me in paths ev - er new.

Refrain.

I will trust in my Sav-ior, I will trust in my Sav-ior, I will

trust in my Sav-ior al - way; He will lead me through the night, By his ev - er shin - ing light, I will trust in my Sav - ior to - day!

No. 130.

McCHESNEY.

"Guide me."

COUNT ZINZENDORF. ♩. = 56 = 50 T. J COOK.

1. Je - sus, guide our way To e - ter - nal day! So shall
2. When we dan - ger meet, Stead - fast keep our feet; Lord, pre-
3. Or - der all our way Through this mor - tal day! In our

we, no more de - lay - ing, Fol - low thee, thy voice o-
serve us un - com - plain - ing, 'Mid the dark - ness round us
toil with aid be near us; In our need with suc - cor

bey - ing; Lead us by the hand To our Fa - ther's land.
reign-ing! Through ad - vers - i - ty Lies our way to thee.
cheer us; When life's course is o'er, O - pen thou the door!

No. 131.

THE WORLD OF JOY.

"For what is your life? It is even a vapor."—James iv: 14.

KELLEY. ♩ = 84 — 20 R. M. McINTOSH.

1. What is life? 'tis but a va - por, Soon it van - ish - es a - way;
2. See that glo - ry, how re - splendent! Brighter far than fan - cy paints;
3. Joy - ful crowds, his throne surrounding, Sing with rapture of his love;
4. Go, and share his peo-ple's glo - ry, 'Midst the ransomed crowd appear;

Life is like a dy - ing ta - per: O, my soul, why wish to stay?
There, in ma - jes - ty tran-scen-dent, Je-sus reigns, the King of saints.
Through the heavens his prais - es sounding, Fill-ing all his courts a-bove!
Thine a joy - ful, wondrous sto - ry, One that an - gels love to hear.

Why not spread thy wings and fly Straight to yon- der world of joy?
Spread thy wings, my soul, and fly Straight to yon- der world of joy,
Spread thy wings, my soul, and fly Straight to yon- der world of joy.
Spread thy wings, my soul, and fly Straight to yon- der world of joy.

Why not spread thy wings and fly Straight to yon - der world of joy?
Spread thy wings, my soul, and fly Straight to yon - der world of joy
Spread thy wings, my soul, and fly Straight to yon - der world of joy.
Spread thy wings, my soul, and fly Straight to yon - der world of joy.

KNOCKING AT THE DOOR.

No. 132.

"Behold, I stand at the door and knock."—Rev. iii: 20.

Mrs. M. B. C. SLADE. $\quad \bullet = 96 = 15\frac{1}{4}$ Dr. A. B. EVERETT.

By permission.

1. Who at my door is stand - ing— Pa - tient - ly draw -ing near,
2. Lone-ly without he's stay - ing— Lone - ly with-in am I;
3. All through the dark hours drear - y, Knock-ing a -gain is he:
4. Door of my heart, I hast - en! Thee will I o - pen wide;

En - trance with- in de-mand - ing? Whose is the voice I hear?
While I am still de - lay - ing, Will he not pass me by?
Je - sus, art thou not wea - ry, Wait - ing so long for me?
Though he re-buke and chast - en, He shall with me a - bide.

Chorus.

Sweet - ly the tones are fall - ing:— "O - pen the door for me,

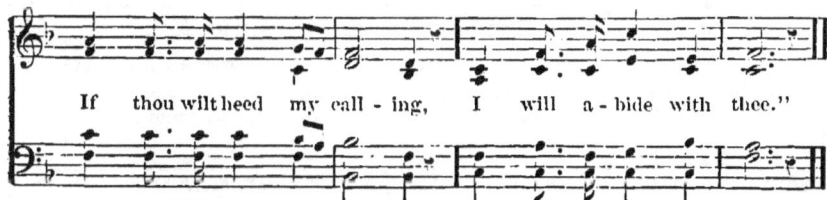

If thou wilt heed my call - ing, I will a - bide with thee."

No. 133.

TRUSTING IN THE PROMISE.

"Come unto me, all ye that labor and are heavy laden, and I will give you rest."—Matt. xi: 28.

Rev. H. B. HARTZLER.   ♩ = 108 = 12   E. S. LORENZ.

1. I have found re - pose for my wea - ry soul, Trust-ing in the
2. I will sing my song as the days go by, Trust-ing in the
3. O the peace and joy of the life I live, Trust-ing in the

prom - ise of the Sav - ior; And a har - bor safe when the
prom - ise of the Sav - ior; And re - joice in hope while I
prom - ise of the Sav - ior; O the strength and grace on - ly

bil - lows roll, Trust-ing in the prom - ise of the Sav - ior. I will
live or die, Trust-ing in the prom - ise of the Sav - ior. I can
God can give, Trust-ing in the prom - ise of the Sav - ior. Who - so-

fear no foe in the dead-ly strife, Trust-ing in the prom-ise of the
smile at grief and a - bide in pain, Trust-ing in the prom-ise of the
ev - er will may be saved to - day, Trust-ing in the prom-ise of the

Sav - ior; I will bear my lot in the toil of life, Trust-ing in the
Sav - ior; And the loss of all shall be high-est gain, Trust-ing in the
Sav - ior; And be-gin to walk in the ho - ly life, Trust-ing in the

Refrain.

prom - ise of the Sav - ior.
prom - ise of the Sav - ior. Rest-ing on his mighty arm for- ev - er,
prom - ise of the Sav - ior.

Nev - er from his lov - ing heart to sev - er, I will rest by grace

in his strong em-brace, Trust-ing in the prom- ise of the Sav - ior.

THE HANDWRITING ON THE WALL.

No. 134.

"And the king saw the part of the hand that wrote."—Dan. v: 5.

K. SHAW.

♩ = 90 = 15¼

KNOWLES SHAW.

1. At the feast of Bel - shazzar and a thou - sand of his lords,
2. See the brave cap -tive Dan-iel as he stood be - fore the throng,
3. See the faith, zeal, and cour-age that would dare to do the right,
4. So our deeds are re - cord-ed—there's a Hand that's writ - ing now;

While they drank from gold-en ves-sels, as the book of truth re-cords,
And re -buked the haughty mon-arch for his might-y deeds of wrong;
Which the Spir - it gave to Dan - iel—this the se - cret of his might;
Sin- ner, give your heart to Je - sus, to his roy - al man-date bow;

In the night as they rev-el in the roy - al pal - ace hall,
As he read out the writing—'twas the doom of one and all.
In his home in Ju - de - a, or a cap - tive in the hall,
For the day is ap-proaching, it must come to one and all,

They were seized with con - ster - na-tion, 'twas the hand up- on the wall.
For the king- dom now was finished, said the hand up- on the wall.
He un - der - stood the writ-ing of his God up- on the wall.
When the sin - ner's con - dem - na-tion will be writ-ten on the wall.

Chorus.

'Tis the hand of God on the wall;　'Tis the hand of God
'Tis the hand of God that is writing on the wall;　'Tis the hand of God

on the wall;　Shall the re-cord be, "Found wanting," or shall it
that is writing on the wall;

be, "Found trusting?" While that hand is writ-ing on the wall,
writ-ing on the wall.

No. 135.

DORRNANCE.

"He careth for you."—1 Pet. v: 7.

HORATIUS BONAR.　　♩ = 60 = 39　　I. B. WOODBURY.

1. Yes, for me, for me he car-eth, With a broth-er's ten-der care;
2. Yes, o'er me, o'er me he watch-eth, Cease-less watch-eth, night and day;
3. Yes, for me he stand-eth plead-ing At the mer-cy-seat a-bove;
4. Yes, in me, in me he dwell-eth; I in him, and he in me;

Yes, with me, with me he shar-eth Ev-ery bur-den, ev-ery fear.
Yes, e'en me, e'en me he snatcheth From the per-ils of the way.
Ev-er for me in-ter-ced-ing, Con-stant in un-tir-ing love.
And my emp-ty soul he fill-eth, Here and through e-ter-ni-ty.

No. 136.

"I AM THE VINE."

"For without me ye can do nothing."—John xv: 1-10.

K. SHAW.   KNOWLES SHAW.

1. I   am the vine, and ye are the branches, Bear precious fruit for
2. Now ye are clean, through words I have spok- en, A-bid - ing in me, much
3. Yes, by your fruits the world is to know you, Walk- ing in love as

Je - sus to - day; The branch that in me no fruit ev - er bear-eth,
fruit ye shall bear; "Dwell - ing in thee, my prom-ise un-brok - en,
children of day; Fol - low your Guide, he passed on be - fore you,

Chorus.

Je - sus hath said, "He tak - eth a - way."
Glo - ry in heaven with me ye shall share." "I am the vine, and
Lead-ing to realms of glo - ri - ous day.

ye are the branches, I am the vine, be faithful and true; Ask what ye

by permission.

Ritard.

will, your prayer shall be granted; The Father loved me, so I have loved thee."

WHEN SHALL WE MEET AGAIN?

No. 137.

"He hath prepared for them a city."—Heb. xi: 16.

Dr. L. MASON.

1. When shall we meet a - gain, Meet ne'er to sev - er? When will peace
2. When shall love free- ly flow, Pure as life's riv - er? When shall sweet
3. Up to that world of light Take us, dear Sav - ior; May we all

wreathe her chain Round us for - ev - er? Our hearts will ne'er re- pose Safe
friend-ship glow,Changeless for- ev - er? Where joys ce - les - tial thrill,Where
there u - nite, Happy for - ev - er: Where kindred spir- its dwell,There

from each blast that blows, In this dark vale of woes— Never—no, never!
bliss each heart shall fill, And fears of parting chill, Never—no, never!
may our mu - sic swell, And time our joys dispel, Never—no, never!

No. 138.

TO CANAAN.

"But now they desire a better country, that is an heavenly."—Heb. xi: 16.

Mrs. M. B. C. SLADE.   ♩ = 100 = 14   Dr. A. BROOKS EVERETT.

1. We are marching to Ca-naan, thro' the desert vast, And the Lord, with cloud by
2. Though we thirst in the des-ert, thou art ev - er nigh, Giv- ing wa- ters, clear and
3. Green and cool E-lim's palm trees, where we peaceful rest, Dewy shelter sweet and
4. When the swell-ing of Jordan sounds up-on the shore, When its parted waves we

day And with light of his presence, till the night is past, Is shin-ing o'er the way.
sweet; If we faint on the journey, manna from on high Is fall-ing at our feet.
fair; There our Shepherd has borne us, on his gentle breast, So lov- ing is his care.
see, We will sing glad hosan-nas, joy- ful passing o'er; We're coming un-to thee.

Chorus.

To Jor - dan when we come, As we cross the bil-low's foam, Come thou o'er its wave, our Guide to be. We are com- ing, com - ing,

lead us safe - ly home, Till the shin-ing land we see.

No. 139.   **HURSLEY.**

"In him was life, and the life was the light of men."—John. i: 4.

J. KEBLE. $\quad = 88 = 18$ W. H. MONK—arr.

1. Sun of my soul! thou Sav - ior dear, It is not night if thou be near;
2. When soft the dews of kind-ly sleep My wearied eyelids gently steep,
3. A-bide with me from morn till eve, For without thee I can not live;
4. Be near to bless me when I wake, Ere through the world my way I take;

O may no earth-born cloud a - rise   To hide thee from thy serv-ant's eyes.
Be my last thought— how sweet to rest   For-ev- er on my Sav - ior's breast!
A-bide with me when night is nigh,   For without thee I dare not die.
A-bide with me till, in thy love,   I lose my- self in heaven a - bove.

SONGS FOR SPECIAL OCCASIONS.

GLORY TO GOD IN THE HIGHEST!

No. 140.

"A multitude of the heavenly host praising God, and saying—"—Luke ii: 13.

F. J. C.

$\textbf{♩} = 112 = 11\frac{1}{4}$

WM. B. BRADBURY.

1. Glo- ry to God in the high - est! Glo- ry to God, glo - ry to God!
2. Glo- ry to God in the high - est! Glo- ry to God, glo - ry to God!

Glo - ry to God in the high - est! Shall be our song to - day;
Glo - ry to God in the high - est! Shall be our song to - day;

Semi-Chorus, or Duet.

An-oth-er year's rich mercies prove His cease-less care and boundless love;
The song that woke the glorious morn When David's great - er Son was born;

(148)

So let our loud-est voic-es raise   Our an- ni- ver- sary song of praise.
Sung by an heavenly host, and we Would join th'an-gel - ic com - pa - ny.

Full Chorus.

Glo - ry to God in the high - est! Glo - ry to God in the high - est!

Glo - ry, glo - ry, glo - ry, glo - ry, Glo - ry be to God on high!

Glo - ry, glo - ry, glo - ry, glo - ry, Glo - ry be to God on high!

No. 141.

CHRISTMAS SONG.

"And suddenly there was with the angel a multitude of the heavenly host praising God."—Luke ii: 13.

HURN.   𝅘𝅥 = 96 = 15¼   S. B. ELLENBERGER.

1. An - gels rejoiced and sweet-ly sung At our Re-deem-er's birth;
2. Glo - ry to God, who dwells on high, And sent his on - ly Son
3. Good-will to men; ye fall - en race! A - rise, and shout for joy;
4. Lord, send the gra-cious tid - ings forth, And fill the world with light;

Mortals, a-wake! let ev - ery tongue Proclaim his match-less worth.
To take a serv-ant's form, and die For e - vils we have done.
He comes, with rich,a- bound-ing grace, To save, and not de - stroy.
That Jew and Gentile, through the earth, May know thy sav - ing might.

By permission.

Chorus.   Chime

Ring the mer - ry, mer - ry, mer - ry, mer - ry Christ-mas bells; Mer-ry,

on,   Chime . . . . . .   on;

mer - ry bells, chime on, chime on, Mer - ry, mer - ry, mer - ry bells, chime on;

Glo - ry, glo - ry, glo - ry, glo - ry be to God who dwells on high;

Good will to men, ye fall - en race, A - rise, and shout for joy.

PERON.

No. 142. "Thou shalt guide me with thy counsel."—Ps. lxxiii: 24.

W. WILLIAMS. ♩=58=42 ANON.

1. { Guide me, O thou great Je - ho - vah, Pilgrim through this barren land;
   I am weak, but thou art might - y, Hold me with thy powerful hand.
2. { O - pen thou the crys-tal fount-ain Whence the heal-ing wa - ters flow;
   Let the fi - ery, cloud-y pil - lar Lead me all my jour-ney through;
3. { When I tread the verge of Jor- dan, Bid the swelling stream di - vide;
   Death of death, and hell's de-struc-tion, Land me safe on Ca-naan's side!

Bread of heav- en, bread of heav - en, Feed me till I want no more.
Strong De-liv- erer, strong De-liv - erer, Be thou still my strength and shield.
Songs of prais-es, songs of prais- es I will ev - er give to thee.

THE DRINK I'LL USE.

No. 143.   "Look not upon the wine."—Prov. xxiii: 31.

Rev. A. W. ORWIG.   ♩ = 96 = 15¼

1. The drink I'll use will not be wine, How-ev - er sparkling it may be;
2. The drink I'll use will not be beer, For e - ven that may bring the woe,
3. The drink I'll use will not be ale, How-ev - er harmless it may seem;
4. The drink I'll use will not be gin, Nor rum, nor brandy, nor old rye;

For, in it lurks the ad-der's sting, Although its fangs I may not see.
The bit - ter sorrows, wound and tear, And lay its tens of thousands low.
That, too, may cause the sad, sad wail, And sink beyond hope's cheering gleam.
For if I do, how dread the thought, The drunkard's death I too may die.

Chorus.

From al - co - hol - - - - - ic poi-son free, ... My drink shall
From al - co - hol, and poi- son free,

pure . . . . cold wa-ter be; . . . . The crystal stream . . . .
My drink shall pure cold wa- ter be; The crys-tal stream

Rit.

that floweth by, ... Shall quench my thirst . . . when I am dry.
that floweth by,   Shall quench my thirst

AMERICA.

No. 144.   "Blessed is the nation whose God is the Lord."—Ps. xxxiii: 12.

S. F. SMITH.   ♩ = 58 = 42   HENRY CAREY.

1. My coun-try! 'tis of thee, Sweet land of lib - er - ty,
2. My na - tive coun - try! thee, Land of the no - ble free,
3. Let mu - sic swell the breeze, And ring from all the trees
4. Our fa - thers' God! to thee, Au - thor of lib - er - ty,

Of thee I sing; Land where my fa - thers died; Land of the
Thy name I love; I love thy rocks and rills, Thy woods and
Sweet free - dom's song; Let mor - tal tongues a - wake, Let all that
To thee we sing; Long may our land be bright With free - dom's

pil- grim's pride; From ev - ery moun - tain side Let free- dom ring.
tem - pled hills; My heart with rap - ture thrills Like that a - bove.
breathe par- take, Let rocks their si - lence break, The sound pro - long.
ho - ly light; Pro - tect us by thy might, Great God, our King!

WAITING AND WATCHING FOR ME.

"For so an entrance shall be ministered unto you abundantly into the everlasting kingdom of our Lord and Savior Jesus Christ."—2 Pet. 1: 11.

KNOWLES SHAW.

By permission.

1. When my fi - nal fare - well to the world I have said, And glad - ly lie
2. There are lit - tle ones glancing a-bout in my path, In want of a
3. There are old and for - sak - en who ling - er awhile In homes which their
4. O should I be brought there by the boun-ti - ful grace Of him who de -

down to my rest; When soft - ly the watchers shall say, "He is
friend and a guide; There are dear lit - tle eyes look-ing up in - to
dear-est have left; And a few gen - tle words or an ac - tion of
lights to for - give; Though I bless not the wea - ry a - bout in my

dead," And fold my pale hands o'er my breast; And when, with my
mine, Whose tears might be eas - i - ly dried; But Je - sus may
love May cheer their sad spir - its be - reft; But the Reap-er is
path, Pray on - ly for self while I live,— Me - thinks I should

glo - ri - fied vis - ion, at last The walls of "That Cit - y" I see,
beckon the children a - way In the midst of their grief and their glee —
near to the long-standing corn, The wea - ry will soon be set free—
mourn o'er my sin - ful neg-lect, If sor - row in heav-en could be,

1-3. Will a - ny   one then   at   the   beau- ti - ful   gate,   Be   waiting   and
4. Should no one   I   love   at   the   beau- ti - ful   gate,   Be   waiting   and

Chorus.

watching   for   me?   Be wait-ing   and watching for me?   . . . . .   Be
watching   for   me;   Be wait-ing   and watching for me;   . . . . .   Be

Be wait-ing   and watching, be wait-ing for me;   Be

wait - ing   and watch-ing   for   me?   . . . .   Will   a - ny   one
wait - ing   and watch-ing   for   me;   . . . .   Should no   one   I

wait- ing   and watching, be watch-ing   for   me;

Rit.

then   at   the   beau- ti - ful   gate,   Be   wait-ing   and watching for   me?
love   at   the   beau- ti - ful   gate,   Be   wait-ing   and watching for   me.

No. 146.

WELCOME.

"Behold, how good and how pleasant it is for brethren to dwell together in unity."—Ps. cxxxiii: 1.

C. C. CLINE.
Chorus.

♩ =100 =41

Har. by C. C. CLINE.

Welcome, welcome, welcome, We welcome you, dear friends, In this our

Fine.

opening lay; Welcome, welcome, welcome, Welcome here this fes - tal day.

By permission.

Duet.

1. Man-y   are   the   sor - rows, man-y   are   the   tears,   Man-y   are   the
2. Man-y   are   the   con - flicts, man-y   are   the snares,   Man-y   are   the
3. Man-y   are   the   pleas-ures that we   here shall share,   Man-y   are   the

joys, and   man - y   are   the   fears   That have crossed our pathway since   we
trials, and   man - y   are   the   cares   That we've borne through Jesus, since we
treas-ures   we must homeward bear,   That we may   be   true   till   we   the

D. C. to Chorus.

last did meet,   But we've come a- gain, our kindred and our friends to greet.
last did meet,   But we're here   a- gain, our brethren and our friends to greet.
Mas-ter meet,   When we'll come a- gain, our loved ones and our friends to greet.

No. 147.   "Hitherto hath the Lord helped us."—1 Sam. vii: 12.

Rev. J. H. MARTIN.   ♩ = 96 = 15¼   Dr. A. B. EVERETT.

1. Praise to the Savior! praise to his name! With tuneful lips his honors proclaim;
2. Praise to the Savior! now let us sing Glad songs and hymns to Jesus our King;
3. Praise to the Savior! let us o-bey, And serve, and fol-low him in the way;

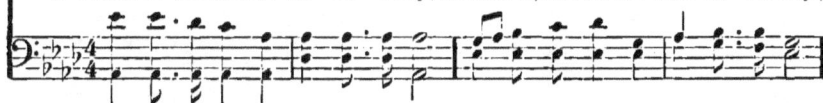

With grate-ful hearts spread widely his fame, Thank-ful-ly bless- ing him.
And let our voic - es joy - ful - ly ring With ech-oes to his name.
He's pres - ent here, he's with us to- day: Ho - san-nas let us raise.

Chorus.

Hap-py, hap-py are our hearts to-day, For the Lord has brought us on our way;

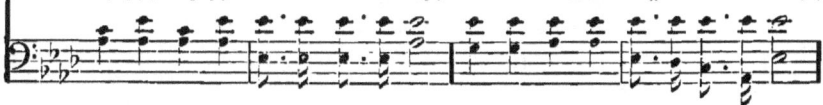

May he to us his grace still dis-play, And bring us safe - ly home!

No. 148.

GOD BE WITH YOU.

"The grace of our Lord Jesus Christ be with you."—1 Cor. xvi: 23.

J. E. RANKIN. $\bullet = 84 = 20$ W. G. TOOMER.

1. God be with you till we meet a-gain; By his counsels guide, uphold you;
2. God be with you till we meet a-gain; 'Neath his wings securely hide you;
3. God be with you till we meet a-gain; When life's perils thick confound you,
4. God be with you till we meet a-gain; Keep love's banner floating o'er you;

With his sheep se-cure-ly fold you, God be with you till we meet a-gain.
Dai-ly man-na still di-vide you, God be with you till we meet a-gain.
Put his arms un-failing round you, God be with you till we meet a-gain.
Smite death's threatening waves before you, God be with you till we meet a-gain.

By permission.

Chorus.

Till we meet, till we meet, Till we meet at Je-sus' feet (till we meet);
Till we meet, till we meet again,

Till we meet, till we meet, God be with you till we meet a-gain.
Till we meet, till we meet again,

INDEX.

(159)